Trust Taxation Manual

Trust Taxation Manual

Brian Courtney, M Com Sc, FCA
Pannell Kerr Forster
Chartered Accountants

London
Butterworths
1986

United Kingdom	Butterworth & Co (Publishers) Ltd 88 Kingsway, LONDON WC2B 6AB and 61A North Castle Street, EDINBURGH EH2 3LJ
Australia	Butterworths Pty Ltd, SYDNEY, MELBOURNE, BRISBANE, ADELAIDE, PERTH, CANBERRA and HOBART
Canada	Butterworths, A division of Reed Inc., TORONTO and VANCOUVER
New Zealand	Butterworths of New Zealand Ltd, WELLINGTON and AUCKLAND
Singapore	Butterworth & Co (Asia) Pte Ltd, SINGAPORE
South Africa	Butterworth Publishers (Pty) Ltd, DURBAN and PRETORIA
USA	Butterworth Legal Publishers, ST PAUL, Minnesota; SEATTLE, Washington; BOSTON, Massachusetts; and AUSTIN, Texas D & S Publishers, CLEARWATER, Florida

British Library Cataloguing in Publication Data

Courtney, Brian
  Trust taxation manual.
  1. Trusts and trustees——England——
  Accounting
  I. Title
  344.2065'9'024657   KD1495

  ISBN 0 406 50330 3

Set in Great Britain by Cold Composition Ltd, Tonbridge, Kent
and printed by Billings of Worcester

Preface

This is a book for the accountant in general practice and those in a similar position – not for the tax expert. The general practitioner is the central character in the field of personal financial planning, and too often he ignores the important place that trusts can play in his work because of the taxation complexities and pitfalls that he knows can be involved.

Nevertheless there is no reason why he should not know enough about trust taxation to enable him to make full use of this important tool in the service that he gives his clients.

And that is what this book seeks to do – to provide the accountant with sufficient practical guidance to enable him to give trusts their proper place in his financial planning service; and that not only covers the questions of what type of trust to set up and when, but the continuing problems of the trusts' investments and management generally. None of these questions can be answered without first considering the taxation consequences. The accountant who cannot confidently make use of trusts deprives the clients of many opportunities to plan their financial affairs to better advantage.

All the tax rates, allowances and exemptions used are those applying in 1986/87. The law is that applying at 1 August 1986.

Brian Courtney
Pannell Kerr Forster

Contents

Table of statutes

References in the right-hand column are to paragraph and page numbers. Numbers printed in italic type refer to pages of the Appendices.

Table of cases

References in the right-hand column are to paragraph and page numbers. Numbers printed in italic type refer to pages of the Appendices.

Abbreviations

CGT	Capital gains tax
CGTA 1979	Capital Gains Tax Act 1979
FA (year)	Finance Act (year)
IHT	Inheritance tax
IHTA 1984	Inheritance Tax Act 1984
PET	Provisionally exempt transfer
PETA	Pure endowment and a term assurance plan
TA 1970	Income and Corporation Taxes Act 1970
TIA 1961	Trustee Investment Act 1961
TMA 1970	Taxes Management Act 1970
USM	Unlisted Securities Market

Acknowledgments

To Charles Parkinson, Duncan Graham and Moira Duggan of Pannell Kerr Forster and Butterworths for all their help.

Chapter 1 Introduction and Legal Background

1.1   WHAT IS A TRUST?

1.1:1   A trust exists where the legal and equitable interests in property are separated. The settlor gives the legal interest to the trustees and the equitable interest to beneficiaries. The three parties are not mutually exclusive – the settlor may also be a trustee or a beneficiary – a beneficiary may be a trustee – but their roles are distinct. Beneficiaries need not be individuals – they may, for example, be animals or charities.

1.1:2   A trust can be created in many ways. Where an agreement fails there may be an *implied trust* to hold property or funds for the benefit of the original owner. Where property is purchased by one person in the name of another there may be *an implied and resulting* trust in favour of the purchaser. Where a trust fails due to uncertainty or impossibility or illegality there may be a *resulting trust* in favour of the settlor. Where a trustee makes a profit there may be a *constructive trust* in favour of his beneficiary. A person knowingly receiving trust property becomes a constructive trustee of that property.

The more normal *express trust* can even be set up verbally provided the terms are clear.

1.1:3   However, the wise financial advisor will not rely on any of the above legal rules. He will make sure that a proper deed of trust is drawn up, and that the deed sets out clearly what is to be held and by whom it is to be held and for whose benefit it is to be held and on what terms and conditions.

1.1:4   He will also make sure that the subject matter of the trust is legally transferred to the trustees, and this may require a document in addition to the trust deed. If it is land, a legal conveyance is required; if it is shares a form of share transfer is required; if chattels an act of delivery and so on. In most cases the trust will not be enforceable until this is done, although the courts will enforce a trust if the settlor has done all that he can to vest the property but some other party is at fault.

If exceptionally the settlor is to be the sole trustee, the assets will already be vested in him and a declaration in the trust deed is all that is required.

1.1:5   For the trust deed itself to be valid it must contain the 'three certainties' laid down in *Knight v Knight* (1840) 3 Beau 148.

(a) *Certainty of words*   It must be clear that the settlor intended to create a trust. An expressed hope or desire is not enough.

(b) *Certainty of the subject matter* It must be clear what assets are being settled and what interests are being created in those assets.

(c) *Certainty of the objects* There must be beneficiaries who could enforce the trust and it must be clear who they are. A charitable trust is exceptional in that it need not be enforceable by beneficiaries.

1.1:6 A trust is distinguished from other similar legal concepts as follows:

(a) *An agency* will come to an end when the agent dies or resigns and the agent has no legal title to assets.

(b) *A bailment* also does not pass the title in the assets to the bailee and he is bound to return them to the bailor in due course.

(c) *A contract* gives valuable consideration while a trustee cannot benefit from his position. There is no third party to enforce a contract (ie no beneficiary).

(d) *A power of appointment* need not be exercised while a trustee must exercise his duties.

1.1:7 Any person who can own and dispose of an asset can create a valid trust of that asset. But it should be noted that:

(a) A trust created by a minor can be set aside by him when he comes of age.

(b) A trust created by a mentally disabled person can be set aside if the court is satisfied that he did not know what he was doing.

1.2 WHY SET UP A TRUST?

1.2:1 Trusts may be set up for reasons which have little or nothing to do with taxation – for example:

(a) To hold property for minors.

(b) To enable a. beneficiary to enjoy the income but to have no recourse to the capital.

(c) To preserve capital for the next generation.

(d) To provide flexibility regarding future needs or contingencies.

(e) To protect capital in the event of the beneficiary's financial difficulty or bankruptcy.

(f) To hold funds for a (mentally) disabled person.

(g) To hold shares for employees.

(h) To hold funds for charitable purposes, or for pensions, or for historic buildings.

1.2:2   While the above are not basically tax-saving purposes, those under (e) to (h) are given special tax exemptions.

1.2:3   On the other hand many trusts are formed primarily for tax-saving reasons – in cases where the settlor will not or cannot make an absolute gift. The most common reasons are to take the income out of the settlor's higher rates of income tax or to take the capital out of the settlor's estate for IHT. Other tax objectives and how to use trusts in their achievement are set out in Chapter 7.

1.3   LEGAL RESTRICTIONS

There are rules which trusts must observe if they are not to be void or voidable – in general terms they must not be illegal, immoral or contrary to public policy. The main specific rules are set out in the following paragraphs.

1.3:1   The rule against perpetuities

The settlor cannot make his trust last indefinitely – within a limited time the assets must come into the beneficial ownership of a person who can dispose of them.

The trust deed (or will) can specify any period before the vesting provided it is less than 80 years. Failing such a provision in the deed the period is the lifetime of a person conceived before the date of the deed (or the date of death) plus 21 years. When the trust is set up it may not be clear whether the vesting date will obey this second rule, but if it is possible that it may do so, then the trustees may await the outcome.

If the time limit expires before the vesting or if it becomes certain that it will do so, the assets revert to the settlor.

1.3:2   Rules limiting accumulations

This is a different problem because a vesting may take place after a life interest rather than after a period of accumulation. The alternative limits to a period of accumulation are:
(a) The life of the settlor.
(b) Twenty-one years from the settlement date.
(c) The minority of any person conceived at the settlement date, whether a beneficiary or not.

(d) The minority of a beneficiary whether or not alive at the settlement date, provided the rule against perpetuities is not broken, and provided he would be entitled to the income if he were of age.
Note that the settlement date can be the date of death of the settlor.
Note also that where the deed provides for a too-long accumulation, the period will be restricted to the shortest of the above and subsequent accumulation will be void.

1.3:3   Rules protecting creditors

A gift into trust is voidable if it is made:
(a) with the intention to defraud creditors;
(b) within two years before the settlor's bankruptcy;
(c) within ten years before the settlor's bankruptcy, unless the beneficiaries can prove that the settlor was solvent immediately after the gift into trust.
But a transfer into trust is not voidable if it is made:
(d) in good faith and for valuable consideration; or
(e) in consideration of marriage.

1.3:4   Rules protecting settlors

A gift into trust may be set aside if it has been:
(a) made in ignorance or in error;
(b) procured by fraud, duress or undue influence.

1.3:5   Rules protecting family life

A trust is void if it is designed:
(a) in total restraint of marriage;
(b) to separate husband and wife;
(c) to separate parent and child.

1.4   TRUSTEES

1.4:1   The appointment of trustees

Any adult who can hold property can be appointed a trustee as can a trust corporation and similar persons. The court may remove from trusteeship, a bankrupt or a criminal.

In the case of a new trust the settlor may appoint the trustees (who can include himself) or may empower some other person to make the appointment. If the settlor fails to do so or if the persons appointed refuse to act, the court may appoint trustees.

In the case of an existing trust, additional trustees or replacement trustees may be appointed as provided in the trust deed and failing such provision by the existing trustees and failing them by the representatives of the last surviving trustee and failing them by the court.

Persons able to appoint trustees cannot appoint themselves. Additional trustees cannot be appointed if they would bring the number above four nor if the sole existing trustee is a trust corporation.

Replacement trustees may be required where an existing trustee ceases to act for any reason (death, incapacity, absence, liquidation etc).

Existing trustees must do all in their power to vest the trust assets in the future trustees.

A person appointed trustee does not have to accept the appointment, but if he acts as trustee in any way he has accepted and if he signed the trust deed as trustee he has accepted. He then remains a trustee as long as he lives or as long as the trust lasts or until he retires or is removed. But he can only retire or be removed in accordance with the trust deed or with the court's consent or on the appointment of a replacement under the Trustee Act 1925, s 36 or under the rather restrictive provisions of s 39.

Land cannot be held by more than four trustees nor less than two, and as mentioned above, additional trustees cannot be appointed to bring the number above four, nor can a trustee retire if that would only leave one trustee (not a trust corporation). Subject to the foregoing there is no general rule about the number of trustees who may be appointed.

1.4:2   The duties of trustees

In the absence of provision to the contrary in the trust deed, a trustee has the following duties:

(a) He must exercise the same care that a businessman would give to his own affairs. If he is a paid trustee the standard is higher in accordance with his professional skill.

(b) He must not profit from his position nor purchase trust property nor receive remuneration (and this may include directors' fees). He is however entitled to recover trust expenses and the trust deed or the court may allow him remuneration.

(c) He must keep proper accounts and other records, and allow the beneficiaries to examine them.

(d) He must act personally and not delegate his duties except as allowed by the trust deed or the Trustee Act 1925.

(e) He must act jointly with his co-trustees. This involves (inter alia) unanimous decisions and joint cheque signing.

(f) He must act strictly in accordance with the trust deed unless the court has varied the terms.

(g) He must pay the proper amounts (either of capital or income) to the beneficiaries and will be personally liable if funds go to the wrong person.

(h) He must invest the trust funds as authorised by the trust deed or the Trustee Investments Act 1961 and hold a balance between the interests of life tenant and remainderman.

1.4:3 The powers of trustees

The duties of trustees involve certain powers and others may be provided by the trust deed. Others again are conferred by the Trustee Act 1925 unless any of them are specifically excluded by the trust deed. These are provided by ss 12-32 as follows:

(a) The power to sell property or to postpone sale and meantime to mortgage or manage it.

(b) The power to give valid receipts but subject to the need for two trustees to deal with land.

(c) The power to settle liabilities and claims, to deal with debts by postponing, compounding or abandoning them.

(d) The power to insure property against fire up to three-quarters of its value. (The trust deed may of course impose a duty to keep it fully insured).

(e) The power to deposit documents for safekeeping.

(f) The power to get in the reversion at the end of an interest in possession by agreeing values or obtaining transfers of property or whatever other action is required.

(g) The power to reimburse themselves for trust expenses paid or incurred.

(h) The power to make provision out of income for the maintenance of beneficiaries whether their interest is vested or contingent, provided the trust deed does not dispose of the income otherwise.

(i) The power to advance up to half the capital in which a beneficiary has a vested or contingent interest, provided no beneficiary's prior interest is prejudiced without his consent in writing.

1.4:4   Beneficiaries and trustees

In the normal course of events a beneficiary cannot interfere in the administration of the trust by the trustees but this is subject to certain exceptions:

(a) Where a breach of trust has occurred or is about to occur, beneficiaries can take legal action to rectify or prevent the breach.

(b) Where all the beneficiaries are of full age and not under any disability they can agree to vary the terms of the trust. This is normally done by a 'deed of family arrangement'.

(c) Where all the beneficiaries are of full age and not under any disability and are absolutely entitled to the trust assets they can terminate the trust (*Saunders v Vautier* (1835-42) All ER Rep 58).

(d) A single beneficiary of full age and not under any disability can surrender his interest (eg his life interest or reversionary interest) or assign it to another or merge it with another interest.

(c) Where there is a beneficiary under a disability or not of full age any arrangement affecting his interest must be approved by the court under the Variation of Trusts Act 1958.

Thus the powers and duties of the trustees should be read as subject to these exceptions.

1.5   TRUSTEE INVESTMENTS

1.5:1   As mentioned in **1.4:2** (h) trustees have a duty to invest the trust funds as authorised by the trust deed or, failing such provision, as authorised by the Trustee Investments Act 1961. The Act does not authorise certain common investments and so trustees can only hold these if they are part of the original settlement or if the deed otherwise provides for them. These omitted investments include:

(a) land;

(b) shares in private companies;

(c) shares and debentures in non-UK companies;

(d) off-shore unit trusts;

(e) unauthorised unit trusts.

On the other hand, many trust deeds forbid investment in eg undated fixed interest stocks.

The investments authorised by the Act are divided into 'narrower-range' and 'wider-range' investments.

1.5:2 Narrower-range investments

National savings bonds
National savings certificates } These are the only items not requiring professional advice.
Savings bank deposits
British government (fixed interest) stocks.
British local authority stocks, bonds and short-term deposits.
Stocks of certain statutory undertakings (gas and water etc).
Loans on first mortgages of land in England, Wales and Northern Ireland up to two-thirds of the property value. The land must be freehold or a leasehold of at least 60 years. The trustees must act on the written advice of an independent surveyor, or valuer.
Deposits with trustee building societies.
Debentures of UK companies subject to the conditions applying to shares (see below).
Special investment deposits in a trustee savings bank.
Fixed interest securities of Commonwealth public authorities or governments (and certain other bodies) quoted on The UK Stock Exchange.

1.5:3 Wider-range investments

Fully paid-up shares issued in the UK by a UK company and listed on The Stock Exchange. The company must have a paid-up capital of at least £1m, and have paid a dividend on all its shares in each of the previous five years.
Shares in trustee building societies.
Units in authorised unit trusts.

1.5:4 Up to half the funds may be in wider-range investments.

1.5:5 Apart from basic national savings both lists of investments require professional advice in writing. This written advice (which the trustees must consider but not necessarily follow) must be from a person whom the trustees reasonably believe qualified to give it.

1.6 DISCRETIONARY TRUSTS

Such trusts give the trustees the power to distribute income or capital (or both) among beneficiaries at their discretion.
  The beneficiaries need not be named if they are a specified class (eg my grandchildren).

The fact that individual shares are not fixed in advance does not offend against the rule that the objects of the trust must be certain.

The main advantages of this type of trust are listed in **1.6:1** to **1.6:4**.

1.6:1   Flexibility

(a) The share of each beneficiary can be varied according to his needs or his tax position.

(b) If the deed does not provide for all the income to be paid out income can be held back and distributed in a later year, or added to capital.

1.6:2   Protection

(a) No beneficiary can claim anything as of right.

(b) A trustee in a beneficiary's bankruptcy cannot make a claim.

1.6:3   Control

(a) The settlor can retain some measure of control by being one of the trustees.

(b) He can also retain the right to appoint income or capital in his will.

1.6:4   Inheritance tax

(a) The trust assets are not aggregated with the assets of the settlor (unless he has retained an interest) or the beneficiaries.

(b) Only lifetime rates are used.

1.6:5   The disadvantages of such trusts (which will be considered later) are:

(a) The beneficiary does not know how he stands with regard to income or capital and so cannot make firm plans.

(b) The beneficiary has no saleable rights.

(c) The income bears investment income surcharge.

(d) The capital suffers periodic charges.

(e) There is no tax-free uplift (for CGT) on a beneficiary's death.

(f) No advantage can be taken of a beneficiary's good IHT position.

1.7 INTRODUCTION TO TRUST TAXATION

1.7:1 The trustees of a settlement are treated for tax purposes as a single and continuing body of persons separate from the individuals who from time to time are trustees. This has the following consequences:

(a) Their tax affairs as trustees are entirely separate from their tax affairs as individuals.
(b) A change in the persons who are the trustees of a particular settlement does not give rise to a disposal for CGT, a transfer for IHT, or a break in continuity for income tax purposes.
(c) A transfer by an individual personally to himself as trustee will normally give rise to all of these things even if he has some beneficial interest in the trust.

1.7:2 This complete separation of the trust's tax affairs from the personal tax affairs of the trustee is not however repeated when it comes to the beneficiary, because there are a number of instances where the tax positions of trust and beneficiary are related. For example, where trust assets subject to a life interest become liable to IHT, it is the tax position of the life tenant which determines the trust's tax liability. Similarly the income tax position of a beneficiary (eg a non-resident) can sometimes affect the trust's income tax affairs.

1.7:3 Moreover, all through the trust's tax affairs there stalks the ghost of the settlor, visiting on his trustees the consequences of his IHT 'snowball' or his domicile, or his connected persons or his retained interest.

1.7:4 However, it is a good general rule, particularly when no one has a right to the trust income, to regard the trust as a separate taxpayer in its own right.

Chapter 2   Income Tax

13

2.1   INTRODUCTION

A trust is not a body corporate nor is it treated as an unincorporated body and so it is not liable to corporation tax.

On the other hand a trust is not an individual and so it is not entitled to personal allowances or other reliefs available to individuals (Note IT 1) nor is it liable to higher rates of income tax. It is liable to basic rate income tax simply because income is so liable no matter who receives it (TA 1970, ss 68(1), 114 and 94(1)) and this applies even if one beneficiary is entitled to all the income (*Hamilton Russell's Executors v IRC* (1943) 25 TC 200).

Not only is there no deduction for personal allowances, but there is no deduction for expenses — a trust has no equivalent of an investment company's management expenses claim. Some expenses are of course deductible before arriving at the figure of income from certain sources — for example, where a trust has let property there is a deduction for commission, repairs and insurance etc before arriving at the taxable rental income. Similarly, where a trust is carrying on a business, trading expenses are deductible in arriving at the business profit taxable. There can also be tax relief for some interest payments and for trading losses.

In the main however, the trust outgoings are not deductible before charging tax and are dealt with in a separate section (**2.3**).

Some trusts are ineffective for income tax purposes because they have strayed into the orbit of the anti-avoidance provisions. The result is that some or all of the income is treated as the settlor's income and not that of the trust or the beneficiary. These trusts are dealt with at the end of this chapter on income tax (**2.7**).

We look now at the main types of income a trust might receive and at how the basic rate tax is suffered.

2.2   INCOME

2.2:1   Income received in full

(a)   Some interest (eg from the National Savings Bank or from certain gilts or from individuals) is received in full and basic rate tax is payable under Schedule D Case III. Building society deposits over £50,000 for a fixed term not exceeding 12 months and large bank deposits also pay interest in full. In the trust accounts a proportion of the next interest payment may be accrued, but this must be ignored for tax purpose and a 'cash' basis used. Where the interest is credited to a (bank) account, that is equivalent to payment.

(b) Rental income has been referred to above. After deduction of items which the lease imposes on the lessor (perhaps repairs, insurance, management etc) tax is payable under Schedule A.

(c) Trading income has also been referred to above. After deduction of expenses laid out wholly for the purposes of the trade and any capital allowances, the profit is taxable under Schedule D Case I.

(d) Foreign income is taxable under Schedule D Case IV or V and may be any of the above types. It does not matter whether it is received in the UK or not. There is a particular problem arising out of the fact that the income may have suffered foreign tax, and double tax relief may be due. If the foreign tax does not qualify for double tax relief it may be used to reduce the assessible income.

Interest from foreign building societies (including the Irish Republic) is untaxed income and there is no relief for foreign 'composite rate' tax.

2.2:2 Income taxed at source

(a) Other interest (eg on debentures, loan stocks and most gilts) is received with basic rate tax already deducted by the payer.

(b) Annual payments (other than interest) such as annuities or patent royalties are also received with basic rate tax deducted by the payer.

(c) Distributions from unit trusts come under this heading where they distribute a gross amount less income tax rather than an 'actual' amount plus a tax credit.

(d) Foreign dividends and other foreign income may have passed through an agent (eg a bank) in the UK and suffered UK tax. This tax may be at a reduced rate to allow relief for foreign tax and this information should be passed on to the beneficiary in case his personal tax is affected.

2.2:3 Dividends from UK companies

These are received as an 'actual' amount but are entitled to a 'tax credit' (if the trust is resident in the UK) which puts them in the same position as interest received after deduction of tax.

Distributions from unit trusts come under this system where they distribute an 'actual' amount plus a tax credit. Income reinvested in units must be included in the total trust income.

2.2:4　Building society and bank interest

Building society and bank interest is the subject of special arrangements under which the payer accounts for tax at a 'composite rate' and the recipient neither has to pay basic rate tax nor can he recover it if he is not liable. Thus where a trust has such a deposit the certificate of income given to a beneficiary must show separately the amount of this interest included in his share.

The beneficiary can use the actual (net) amount of interest included in his share to cover annual payments which he may make, but he must gross it up at basic rate to calculate his higher rate liability. In no circumstances can he recover the income tax suffered.

Where the trust is liable to investment income surcharge (see Discretionary trusts **2.6:1**) the interest must be grossed up, as in the case of an individual, before making the calculation. But to get credit against tax on income paid out, the deposit must be in a special basic rate (or 'company') account. Building societies maintain such accounts but banks pay interest in full to discretionary trusts and this is assessed under Case III. Large term deposits also pay interest in full — see **2.2:1** (a).

2.2:5　Discretionary income from other trusts

This will be received after deduction of tax at basic rate plus investment income surcharge (see **2.6**). The basic rate tax will come into the calculation of income in the normal way. The surcharge will be set against any liability under FA 1973, s 16 or 17 (**2.6:2** and **2.6:8**) and if there is no such liability it can be reclaimed.

2.2:6　Close company apportionment

Where the trust holds shares in a close company any income of the company apportioned to those shares is part of the trust income for tax purposes and may therefore be part of the beneficiaries income, but only for the purposes of higher rates.

2.2:7 Income from personal representatives

Where income arising during the administration of a deceased's estate is paid by the personal representatives to the trustees this is also part of the trust income for tax purposes and may therefore be part of the beneficiaries' income.

2.2:8 Accrued income scheme

The provisions aimed at 'bondwashing' apply to trusts — see Appendix I Note IT 2.

2.2:9 Offshore income gains

The provisions of FA 1984, Chap VII apply to trusts — see Appendix I Note IT 3.

2.2:10 Other items of income which may arise in trusts and which have special rules are:
— Furnished holiday lettings.
— Sale of patent rights.
— Sale of literary copyright.
— Literary royalties.
— Woodlands managed on a commercial basis.
— Underwriting commissions.
— Premiums on leases.
— Stock dividends.

2.2:11 Investment bonds

Where the trust holds an investment bond (as is common with insurance trusts formed before 18 March 1986) the usual procedure is to withdraw an annual amount not exceeding 5% which may be loaned to the settlor or used to repay a loan by him. Whichever way it is dealt with, the point is that the annual withdrawal is not income of the trust, no tax has to be paid on it and it should not be returned to the Inland Revenue as income. When the bond matures or is surrendered or sold the total gain is calculated (including the annual withdrawals) and there may be a liability on the settlor for higher rate tax, if he is still alive.

There are other problems requiring great care — see 'Excess income distributions' (**2.6:8**) and 'Trusts ineffective for income tax' (**2.7:5**).

This type of investment is also referred to under the heading of 'Insurance trusts' (**5.5:1**) in the chapter on Specialised Trusts. Investment bonds which do produce an income (a temporary annuity) are not suitable for trusts.

2.2:12   Gross trust income

At this stage we can calculate the gross income and the tax suffered (Example **2.8:1**).

2.3   OUTGOINGS

When all the different types of income have suffered basic rate tax (in one way or another) the trust will have certain outgoings which are not deductible in arriving at any of the items of income. These are discussed under four broad headings (see **2.3:1** to **2.3:4**).

2.3:1   Annual payments

The trust may have to make payments from which basic rate income tax has to be deducted under TA 1970, ss 52 and 53. These are called 'annual payments' and the most common are annuities. The terms of the trust may require that before dividing the income between the beneficiaries an annuity of £1,000 per annum is to be paid to some elderly relative. Basic rate tax of £290 is deducted and the net amount of £710 is paid to the annuitant.

The £290 deducted does not have to be paid to the Revenue so long as the tax on the trust income is at least £290. What happens is that the gross trust income is reduced by £1,000 and the tax suffered is reduced by £290 (see Example **2.8:2**).

Where a trustee is entitled under the deed to annual remuneration, this is another example of a charge payable under deduction of basic rate income tax. Where however the trustee is a professional man entitled under the deed to charge his fees, these will not be an annual payment but an expense payable in full which comes under **2.3:4** below.

Other annual payments such as royalties or rent charges rarely arise in a trust.

Where, exceptionally, trustees are directed to pay an annuity (or other annual payment) out of capital, income tax at basic rate is still deductible but has to be passed on to the Inland Revenue in addition to the tax on income.

2.3:2 Interest payments

A trust is in the same position as an individual in that interest is payable in full (unless the recipient is non-resident) and only attracts tax relief in certain restricted circumstances. These circumstances are as follows:

(a) The interest is payable in respect of a period of one year from the making of a loan for the purpose of paying IHT charged on the death of the settlor. The loan must be so applied before the grant of probate. If the estate income is insufficient the excess interest may be carried forward.

(b) The settlor was entitled to tax relief before his death in respect of interest on a house purchase (or improvement) loan and at the time the interest is paid the property is the sole or main residence of the widow/er or a dependant relative.

   A trust does not qualify for tax relief under the MIRAS scheme.

(c) The interest is on a loan for the purchase or improvement of property let at a commercial rent. Such interest is allowable at a Schedule A Assessment only, but if the net rents are insufficient the excess interest may be carried forward.

Other reliefs for interest (purchase of shares, purchase of plant, purchase of a life annuity etc) do not apply to trusts.

As in the case of an individual, overdraft interest is not eligible nor is short interest not to a bank etc. Where the trust pays interest not eligible for tax relief, it is treated as an expense (see **2.3:4**).

2.3:3 Allocations of income

Then there may be payments required by the terms of the trust from which the trustees cannot deduct income tax and for which they cannot claim tax relief. For example, the deed may direct the trustees to pay the premiums on a life insurance policy or to make payments towards redemption of a mortgage. These are payments which reduce the income available for the beneficiaries but which do not come under either of the above heads and are not trustee's expenses.

Such payments are not made out of gross income but out of the net 'after-tax' income. They are relatively rare (see Example **2.8:3**).

This heading does not cover any income which is accumulated or becomes the income of a beneficiary.

2.3:4 Trustees' expenses

Lastly we have those expenses which are not deductible in arriving at the income from any particular source, and which are not annual payments nor allocations of income. They will commonly include accountants' and solicitors' fees, postage, stationery, bank charges and perhaps overdraft interest. Basically they are the costs of administering the trust and collecting the income.

Like the allocations of income these are paid out of the net and not the gross income. In other words they reduce the net cash available for the beneficiaries (Example **2.8:3**).

The authority for the reduction of the beneficiaries' statutory income by expenses is the case of *Macfarlane v IRC* (1929) 14 TC 532.

For non-deductible expenses see Appendix I Note IT 4.

2.4 TREATMENT OF THE NET TRUST INCOME

Having arrived at the net income available for distribution or otherwise the next stage divides sharply into two alternatives depending on whether the beneficiary is or is not absolutely entitled to that net income. Looked at from the other side — must the trustees distribute the income or have they the right to withhold it or (which has the same effect) a duty to accumulate it?

Where a beneficiary is absolutely entitled to the income it is his for tax purposes year by year as it arises. Such a trust is known as a fixed interest trust.

Where he is not so entitled, income only becomes his for tax purposes when the trustees pay it to him or for his benefit. This is subject to an exception where income is accumulated for a beneficiary until the happening of a contingency (eg his coming of age); if the accumulated income is then paid to him it is not his income but part of the trust capital. Nor can the Revenue (or the beneficiary) go back to treat it as his income year by year as it arose. This is because in the event of his dying before becoming entitled, the accumulated income would not go to his estate but would pass with the capital under the Trustee Act 1925, s 31.

Thus the tax treatment of the net income can change from time to time — for example, the beneficiary may have no absolute right to the income until he comes of age but have such a right thereafter. The two regimes may even exist side by side at the same time — one beneficiary being absolutely entitled to part of the income while another is not so entitled (eg because he has not come of age).

So we look first of all at the case of a 'fixed interest' or 'interest in possession' and secondly, at the cases where there is no such interest either because the trustees have discretion what to do with the income or because they have a duty to accumulate it.

2.5 THE BENEFICIARY WITH A FIXED INTEREST

2.5:1 General

The net income arrived at above is divisible among those entitled to it (Example **2.8:4**) and the individual beneficiary's share (one-half or one-quarter or whatever) is grossed up at 29% to arrive at that beneficiary's statutory income from the trust. The exception is 'composite rate' interest from a bank or building society which is dealt with separately at its actual net amount. The beneficiary is entitled to a certificate of his income and this is provided by the trust on Form R185E (Example **2.8:5**).

As well as composite rate interest, the certificate should also show separately items of income which have suffered reduced rates of tax because of relief for foreign tax (Example **2.8:6**).

The beneficiary's share is treated in his hands just like any other form of income which has borne (or been credited with) basic rate or reduced rate tax. The beneficiary can recover tax or pay more depending on his personal tax position but the trustees are not concerned with that. Again 'composite rate' interest is exceptional in that the tax cannot be recovered.

Just because a beneficiary is entitled to the income does not mean that all payments to him are treated as his income. If the trustees have power to advance capital to him, they can do so without affecting his income tax position.

2.5:2 Beneficiary's exempt income

It is possible in a certain set of circumstances for the trustees to use a beneficiary's tax exemption to avoid paying tax which the beneficiary can immediately reclaim (*Reids Trustees v IRC* (1929) 14 TC 512).

This occasion arises when a beneficiary is entitled to all the income and he is resident outside the UK. Income arising outside the UK and interest from 'exempt gilts' would not be taxable in his hands and the trust can agree with the inspector of taxes to 'short circuit' the system and not pay tax on these items or to receive the interest in full as the case may be. The tax certificate supplied to the beneficiary would have to show these items separately.

It may even be sensible to sell those trust investments which produce income taxable in the hands of a non-resident, and reinvest in others which do not.

Where a non-resident beneficiary is only entitled to a fractional share of the income it is not normally possible for the trust to use his tax exemptions, but a detailed certificate of his share of the income will enable him to make his own claim to repayment. Where a DT agreement provides that 'other income' shall be taxable only in the country of residence, the Revenue will repay all the tax on that share (SP3/86).

2.5:3   Income paid direct

It is sometimes sensible for the trustees to mandate dividends and interest to the beneficiary — this could happen when the beneficiary is entitled to all the trust income, and can save time and trouble and expense. The case of *Williams v Singer* (1921) 7 TC 409 is authority for the proposition that the Revenue cannot assess the trustees, where the income is paid direct to the beneficiary. The trustees are however required to make a return to the Inland Revenue of income paid direct under their authority (TMA 1970, s 76).

2.5:4   Beneficiary entitled to capital

In the exceptional case where a beneficiary has an irrevocable right to part of the capital as well as its income, his share of the trustees' expenses has to be added to his income because he is not entitled to this deduction. Such capital and its income are not 'in trust' for income tax purposes. This can of course be to his advantage if he is able to claim a full tax repayment.

2.6   DISCRETIONARY TRUSTS

2.6:1   General

Different considerations arise where no beneficiary is currently entitled to the income. In these trusts the income only becomes the income of a beneficiary if the trustees exercise their discretion and pay income to him or when they decide to do so. Where the trustees do so the amount of the payment 'grossed up' is the income of the beneficiary, and we will see later that this 'grossing' is at a special rate.

Thus it is possible that little or even no income will be returned by beneficiaries and become liable to higher rates. In these circumstances the response of the tax legislation is to impose investment income surcharge on all the income over which the trustees have discretion or power to accumulate (FA 1973, s 16). Nor does this apply only to large professionally managed trusts; unit trust and other schemes have resulted in large numbers of small accumulation trusts for children being set up, and these too are liable. Income will escape the surcharge if it is not accumulated and not subject to the trustee's discretion. For example, it has to be paid out as a charge or as a specific allocation of income or an expense etc (see **2.6:2**).

2.6:2   Calculation of the surcharge

The trustees are required to make an additional return on Part A of Form 32 arriving at the amount of surcharge payable by deducting from the gross income:
(a) The gross charges.
(b) The gross allowable interest payments.
(c) The 'grossed-up' allocations of income.
(d) The 'grossed-up' expenses.
(e) Any income 'deemed' to be the settlor's income (see 'Ineffective trusts' – **2.7** below).
(f) Any income to which a beneficiary has a right.
The calculation is set out in Example **2.8:7**.

2.6:3   Items included

FA 1973, s 16 provides that the income subject to surcharge includes:
(a) Income apportioned to the trust from a close company under FA 1972, Sch 16, para 1. Where this apportionment is followed by an actual dividend there is the same relief that an individual would receive.
(b) any sum representing liable income paid by the personal representatives of a deceased person to the trustees.

2.6:4   Items excluded

The surcharge does not apply to items which are capital profits under trust law (although income tax is charged on them) and are not specifically charged by s 16:
(a) Premiums treated as rent (TA 1970, s 80).
(b) Profits on sale of certificates of deposit (FA 1973, s 26).
(c) Shares and other capital items treated as company distributions (TA 1970, s 233).

2.6:5   The beneficiary's income

In the case of discretionary trusts instead of dividing the net income between the beneficiaries, the payments to them are grossed up to arrive at their statutory income. This is not the normal grossing-up process because the income has borne basic rate tax plus the surcharge. At current rates this means 29% plus 16% or a total of 45% so that the payment to the beneficiary is 55% of the gross. Thus a payment of £100 will become a gross income of £182 (in other trusts a gross income of £182 is a net payment of £129) and the certificate which the trustees give the beneficiary on Form R185 (1973) will show a gross income of £182 and tax at 45% of £82.

The end result to the beneficiary is the same however, because he will recover tax or pay more on the gross income of £182 depending on whether he is liable to more or less than 45%. As before, this is not the concern of the trustees. The Form R185 (1973) is shown in Example **2.8:8**. The problem of a beneficiary not being able to reclaim 'composite rate' tax does not arise with a discretionary trust because such a trust needs a basic rate tax certificate and therefore a 'company account' (see **2.6:8**).

2.6:6   Payments out of capital

Such payments can be treated as the beneficiary's income if they provide a benefit of an income nature eg maintenance or school fees (*Cunard's Trustees v IRC* (1946) 27 TC 122). This can give rise to an additional tax liability on the trustees — see 'Excess income distributions' (**2.6:8** below). Where the beneficiary has no entitlement to income the position is less certain (*Stevenson v Wishart* (Times 4/1/86)).

2.6:7 Beneficiary's 'look-through' relief

It is possible in certain circumstances for the beneficiary to 'look-through' the discretionary payments to the actual source of income, if that would be to his advantage. For example, where the trust has overseas income the trustees can certify the proportion included in the discretionary payment and so enable the beneficiary to claim double tax relief if his tax rate entitles him to do so. Similarly, if the income includes interest on certain government stocks and the beneficiary is non-resident, a certificate from the trustees of the proportion included in the discretionary payment will enable the beneficiary to reclaim the appropriate tax. Again overseas income would be exempt if it had been received direct by a non-resident and this is dealt with on the 'look-through' basis by virtue of Extra Statutory Concession B 18.

For non-resident beneficiaries affected by double tax agreement see Appendix I Note IT 17.

There is a practical difficulty of identifying income where it has been accumulated and distributed later. The claim goes out of date six years after the end of the year in which the income arose to the trust and not the year of distribution (See Example **2.8:10**).

2.6:8 Excess income distributions

Where trustees exercise their discretion to make distributions they are liable to basic rate tax plus surcharge on the grossed-up distributions subject to allowance for tax already suffered over and above what is required to cover other payments.

The effect of this provision is to collect tax on distributions in excess of net income after outgoings. This calculation is made on a cumulative basis from year to year, and in terms of tax so that tax on an excess of income over payments in any year can be carried forward to cover tax on payments in future years. The calculation is shown in Example **2.8:9** and has to be returned by the trustees to the Revenue on Part B of Form 32. This of course is an anti-avoidance provision and need not concern trustees in normal circumstances.

However, there are several circumstances in which a liability can arise:

(a) Where the trust has income on which tax does not have to be paid (eg on savings certificates or investment bonds). Even if the proceeds of such investments can be regarded as capital, the Revenue will look at the payments to the beneficiary, and if these are of an income nature (eg school fees) tax may have to be paid (*Cunard's Trustees v IRC* (1946) 27 TC 122).

(b) Where payments of an income nature are made out of the normal capital of the trust.

(c) Where payments are made to the beneficiary which could be regarded as capital except that the terms of the trust deed do not allow capital to be paid to him. For example, a loan to a beneficiary will not enter the calculation unless the trustees have no power to make the loan.

(d) Where the income is received in a year of lower tax rates and distributed in a year of higher rates. This is one of those 'one-way-streets' which occur in tax law — there is no compensating advantage if the rates fall rather than rise.

Another problem arises with building society and bank interest which requires a basic rate certificate before credit can be claimed for tax suffered. Such building society deposits therefore have to be in 'company' accounts. Banks do not maintain such accounts and should pay interest to discretionary trusts in full so that it can be assessed direct.

2.7   TRUSTS INEFFECTIVE FOR INCOME TAX

Alienation of income to a trust may result in a loss of tax to the Revenue, and so there are further anti-avoidance provisions the effect of which is to deem the trust income (Appendix I Note IT 5) to be that of the settlor. These are listed below (see **2.7:1** to **2.7:6**).

2.7:1   TA 1970, s 437

Where income is paid for the benefit of an unmarried infant child of the settlor (Appendix I Note IT 6).

2.7:2   TA 1970, s 446

Where capital or income may revert to the settlor or his spouse (Appendix I Note IT 7). This reversion may be as a result of:

(a) a power of revocation or determination or appointment exercisable by any person;

(b) a discretionary power exercisable by any person.

2.7:3 TA 1970, s 447

Where the settlor has retained an interest in the trust property or income (Appendix I Note IT 8). In this case the deeming provision applies to undistributed income only (TA 1970, s 455). Exceptions to this deeming provision are set out in Appendix I Note IT 9.

2.7:4 TA 1970, s 448

Where the settlor has not absolutely divested himself of the trust property. That is to say income or capital may be applied for the benefit of the settlor or his spouse (Appendix I Note IT 10) in any circumstances whatever (Appendix I Notes IT 7 and 9). In this case the deeming provision applies for higher rates only. The income will still be the beneficiary's for basic rate purpose.

2.7:5 TA 1970 ss 451 and 451A

Where a capital sum is paid to the order of the settlor by the trust (Appendix I Note IT 11) or by a connected company (Appendix I Note IT 12) and there is undistributed income (TA 1970, s 455) in the trust (Example **2.8:14**).

2.7:6 Where a settlor has to pay higher rate tax on trust income he may recover it from the trustees because they have control of the income.

2.7:7 It can be seen that there are areas of overlap between these provisions and that is because they were enacted at different times to counter different tax avoidance schemes. One result of this is to give the Revenue a choice as to which provision to rely on, and a second result is to make it very difficult for the taxpayer to put up any defence. It is best to exclude the settlor and his spouse entirely; even to the extent of naming a charity as 'long stop' beneficiary. Although the Revenue lost the case of *Watson v Holland* [1984] STC 372 it illustrates the problem.

This, however, is to look at it from a purely income tax point of view, and there are circumstances in which it is acceptable to have the trust income taxed as that of the settlor to gain other advantages. For example to gain the trust's annual exemption from CGT (£3,150).

2.7:8 Lastly, it should be pointed out that the anti-avoidance provisions are very widely drawn to include 'any . . . agreement, arrangement or transfer of assets' (TA 1970, s 444(2)) and so can catch transactions which would not appear to be trusts. The courts have however sought to place a limit on the scope of the legislation by excluding bona fide commercial transactions; there must be an 'element of bounty' before an arrangement can be a settlement (*IRC v Plummer* (1979) STC 793). The courts will look at the substance of the whole arrangement (including appointments made by the settlor) in applying this 'element of bounty' test (*Chinn v Collins* (1981) STC 1).

Examples of 'arrangements' where the settlement deeming provisions can apply are:

(a) A deed of variation (deed of family arrangement) made within two years of a death to achieve IHT savings or (by election) CGT savings. There is no income tax relief and there may be 'deeming' problems.

(b) A separation agreement on the break-up of a marriage which provides payments for the benefit of unmarried infant children.

2.8 INCOME TAX EXAMPLES

2.8:1 Example IT 1 (see 2.2:12)

	£	£
Rental income net of relevant outgoings	1,800	
Schedule A tax paid		522
Interest received in full	1,900	
Schedule D Case III tax paid		551
Interest received subject to deduction of tax	1,100	
Tax deducted at source		319
	4,800	1,392
Dividends from UK companies (actual)	852	
Tax Credit	348	348
Gross income of trust	6,000	1,740

2.8:2 Example IT 2 (see 2.3:1)

	£	£
Annuity to Auntie Annie	(1,000)	
Tax deducted and retained by trustees		(290)
Interest on loan to improve let property	(500)	
Tax relief by reduction of Schedule A liability		(145)
	4,500	1,305

2.8:3 Example IT 3 (see 2.3:3 and 2.3:4)

	£	£
Gross income *less* charges		4,500
Income tax *less* tax on charges		1,305
		3,195
Net income after tax		
Allocation of income	400	
Trustees' expenses	295	
		695
		2,500

2.8:4   Example IT 4 (see **2.5:1**)

	£	£
After-tax income available for division among the beneficiaries		2,500
Joseph Soap – 50%	1,250	
Fred Bloggs – 20%	500	
Susan Soap – 30%	750	
		2,500

2.8:5 Example IT 5 (see 2.5:1)

Tax Certificate – Beneficiary of Trust *(For use for periods after 5 April 1973 only)*

(If payments are made to the beneficiary at the trustee's discretion, use form R185(1973).)

I Certify that .... JOSEPH SOAP ....

of .... BALLYBACKWARD ....

is a beneficiary of the Trust known as .... THE BILL BLOGGS SETTLEMENT ....

to the extent of (a) .... 50% OF RESIDUAL INCOME .... and the particulars given below are correct.

Information regarding this Trust has been or will be sent to H.M. Inspector of Taxes.

.... LISBURN .... District.   Reference .... B.1234 ....

Signature (b) .... Ima Twitt ....   Date .... 30 June 1987 ....

Address .... 20 GREAT VICTORIA STREET, BELFAST, BT2 7ER ....

Income for the year ended 5 April 19 ... 87 .

Income (c) and (d) (1)	Basic rate tax and/or tax credits relating to the income in column 1 (2)	Net amount of beneficiary's share of Trust income (c) and (d) (3)
£	£	£
1,760 56	510 56	1,250 00

Please do not write in the space below

Notes

(a) Here state whether the beneficiary is entitled to a fixed annual sum or to a fraction of the net income (stating what fraction).

(b) Signature of Trustee or authorised Agent for the Trust.

(c) Do not include capital gains.

(d) Show separately and distinguish in columns (1) and (3) United Kingdom company dividends and dividends or interest from United Kingdom building societies.

R185E (1973)

52.1236 418415.1750M 5/77 HP Ltd

2.8:6   **Example IT 6** (see **2.5:1**)

Tax Certificate – Beneficiary of Trust   *(For use for periods after 5 April 1973 only)*

(If payments are made to the beneficiary at the trustee's discretion, use form R185(1973).)

I Certify that ....

of ....

is a beneficiary of the Trust known as ....

to the extent of (a) .... and the particulars given below are correct.
Information regarding this Trust has been or will be sent to H.M. Inspector of Taxes.

.... District.   Reference.................................

Signature (b) ....   Date ....

Address ....

Income for the year ended 5 April 19........

Please do not write in the space below

Description [Details attached]	Amount of beneficiary's share incl. tax credits on UK Dividends	Tax Deducted or Tax Credit	Provisional credit for Overseas Tax	Net income or actual UK Dividends
	£	£	£	£
UK Dividends				
Income taxed at basic rate				
Income taxed at less than basic rate because of double tax relief				
Untaxed income to be assessed on the beneficiary				
TOTAL				
Deductions [1] Annuities [2] Interest qualifying for relief		*		
TOTAL DEDUCTIONS				
NET INCOME				

Actual interest received under composite rate system	
Trustees expenses	
Actual income	

* This is the gross annuities less the actual composite rate interest
   at basic rate.

2.8:7 Example IT 7 (see **2.6:2**)

This example uses the income and outgoings in Examples IT 1, 2 and 3 but assumes that the residual income is subject to the trustees' discretion.

	£	£
Gross income of Trust		6,000
Less – Charges	1,500	
Allocation of income £400 x 100/71	563	
Trustees' expenses £295 x 100/71	415	
Income deemed to be the settlor's	—	
Income to which a beneficiary has a right	—	
		2,478
		3,522
Investment income surcharge at 16%		564

2.8:8   Example IT 8 (see 2.6:5)

CERTIFICATE OF DEDUCTION OF INCOME TAX *(for payments under Deed of Covenant please use form R185 (AP))*

I certify that on paying to ......JOSEPH SOAP...

of ..........BALLYBACKWARD..

the sum shown in column 3 below, I deducted the amount of income tax shown in column 4, and I further certify that this tax has been or will be paid by me either directly or by way of deduction from other income when received by me.

Signature *(see Note (a))* ....Ima Twitt.. Date .....30 June...... 19 87

Enter here – your private address ▶	299 SANDY ROW, BELFAST 12
Enter here – if you are in business – your business address ▶ *or if you are employed –* the name and address of your employer ▶	22 GREAT VICTORIA STREET BELFAST 2
Name of trust etc. and Tax District and reference *(where applicable)*	THE BILL BLOGGS SETTLEMENT

Nature of the payment e.g. mortgage or loan interest, annuity, rent, payments from a discretionary trust etc. (1)	Profits or other source out of which paid (2)	Gross amount from which I have deducted the tax (3)	Amount of income tax deducted by me *(see Notes (b) and (c))* (4)	Actual amount paid (5)	Period *(i.e. year, half year etc.)* for which the payment was due, date on which due and the actual date of payment in cases referred to in Note (d) below (6)
Payment From Discretionary Trust	General Fund of Trust Income	£ 3,636 : 36	£ 1,636 : 36	£ 2,000 : 00	Date of Payment 20 February 1987

NOTES

(a)   This form should be signed by the person deducting the tax and responsible for accounting for it to the Revenue. Where the person concerned is deducting the tax on behalf of his employer, e.g. as secretary, cashier, etc. this should be stated.

(b)   This form should not be used where income tax has not in fact been deducted from the gross amount payable.

(c)   In the case of a payment made by Trustees of a discretionary trust in exercise of their discretion, enter in column 5 the actual amount paid, in column 4 the amount of tax treated as deducted at a rate equal to the basic rate and the higher additional rate for the year of payment, and in column 3 the corresponding gross amount i.e. the total of the amounts in columns 4 and 5.

(d)   Where any payment is made upon the exercise of a trustee's discretion or in arrear, enter the actual date of payment(s).

Please do not write in the spaces below

"I.R." stamp

"Duty assessed" stamp

R185(1973)

Dd 0552415 500M 4/79 UPS

2.8:9   Example IT 9 (see **2.6:8**)

Using the income and outgoings as before and assuming discretionary
payments of £2,000

	£
Tax brought forward (on accumulated income of previous years)	500
Basic rate tax on income subject to discretion £3,570 @ 30%	1,021
Investment income surcharge (Example **2.8:7**)	564
	2,085
Less credit for foreign tax (DTR)	—
	2,085
Tax on discretionary payments £2,000 x 45/55	1,636
Tax carried forward to next year	449

Note A negative figure will represent a tax liability

2.8:10   Example IT 10 (see **2.6:7**)

Suppose the calculation in Example **2.8:8** is for the year 1986/87 and
the tax brought forward is from 1985/86.

Suppose further that the gross trust income of each year includes
£1,000 interest on 9% treasury loan 1999.

Proportion of income (and tax) represented by exempt gilt.

$$1986/87 \quad \frac{1000}{6000} \quad \text{(See Example 2.8:7)}$$

$$1985/86 \quad \frac{1000}{5000} \quad \text{(Say)}$$

Tax on discretionary payment £1,636 (See Example **2.8:8**).

	£			£
Tax forward from 1985/86	500	x	$\dfrac{1000}{5000}$ =	100
Balance from 1986/87	$\dfrac{1136}{1636}$	x	$\dfrac{1000}{6000}$ =	189
Tax on distributed part of exempt gilt				289

reclaimable by non-resident beneficiary who received the whole discretionary payment of £2,000. If he received part only then the same
proportion of the tax of £289 is reclaimable. If no discretionary
payments were made till 1993/94 the tax would be out of date for a
claim.

2.8:11   Example IT 11 (see **5.1:2**)

Where there is a fixed interest in half the trust income and the other half is subject to the trustee's discretion.

	£	£
Gross income per Example **2.8:1**		6,000
Net income available per Example **2.8:3**	2,500	
Joseph Soap	1,250	
Gross equivalent 100/71	1,760	
Other deductions per Example **2.8:7**	2,478	
		4,238
		1,762
Investment income surcharge 16%		282

2.8:12   Example IT 12 (see **6.2:7**)

In an overseas fixed interest trust the outgoings have to be apportioned between the liable and non-liable income to arrive at the statutory income of a non-resident beneficiary (the statutory income of a resident beneficiary includes all classes of income).

	£
Net liable income per Example **2.8:13**	3,000
UK income tax per Example **2.8:13**	580
	2,420
Proportion of outgoings per Example 12	300
	2,120
Beneficiary's fixed interest (say) 50%	1,060
Less share of actual UK dividend	500
	560
Tax thereon at 29/71	229
Share of actual UK dividend	500
Income on which any higher rate liability would be calculated	1,289

2.8:13   Example IT 13 (see **6.2:7**)

In an overseas discretionary trust the outgoings have to be apportioned between liable and non-liable income to arrive at the investment income surcharge.

	Gross £	*UK Tax* £
Income not liable to UK tax		
Overseas rents	2,000	—
Overseas dividends	2,000	—
	4,000	—
Income liable to UK tax		
UK rents	2,500	725
UK dividends — actual	1,000	—
— tax credit	—	—
	3,500	725
Interest on loan to improve UK let property	500	
Tax relief by reduction of Schedule A liability		145
	3,000	580

	£
Other annual payments (net) or allocations	425
Expenses	250
	700

Proportion relating to UK
liable income $\dfrac{3000}{4000 + 3000}$ = 300

Grossed at 100/71	423
	2,577
Investment income surcharge @ 16%	412

2.8:14 Example IT 14 (see 2.7 :5 and Appendix I Note IT 11)

		£	£
Gross trust income for 1986/87			10,000
Less — Charges (including allowable interest)		1,500	
Allocations of income £400 x $\dfrac{100}{71}$		563	
Expenses £260 x $\dfrac{100}{71}$		366	

Non-allowable
  interest   £490   x $\frac{100}{71}$ 690

Income deemed to be the settlor's under
  other provisions of Part XVI   —
Income to which a beneficiary has right
  (even if not paid out)   —

                                                            3,119

                                                            6,881

Investment income surcharge at 16%   1,101
Income tax at 29%   1,995

                                                            3,096

                                                            3,785

Discretionary payments of income
  (but not to a connected company or a
  connected trust)   2,000

                                                            1,785

Add   Proportion of non-allowable interest
            £490   x $\frac{1785}{3785}$ 231

'Available' income for 1986/87   2,016
'Available' income forward from previous years
  from settlement date (or 6 April 1938)   5,000

                                                            7,016
Loan to settlor in 1986/87   10,000

Balance of loan to be 'matched' with 'available'
  income of future years up to 1996/97   2,984

Addition to settlor's income of 1986/87 (net) 7,016
Gross equivalent £7,016   x $\frac{100}{55}$ 12,756

Chapter 3   Capital Gains Tax

3.1   **INTRODUCTION**

At its most basic level CGT is payable at 30% when a chargeable asset (Appendix II Note CGT 1) is disposed of (Appendix II Note CGT 2) at a profit. The refinements of this general principle are discussed below (see **3.1:1** to **3.1:15**)

3.1:1   Where the asset has not been acquired or disposed of at arms' length, the acquisition or disposal is deemed to be at market value.

3.1:2   The 'cost' of the asset can be index-linked from the date of acquisition (or from March 1982 if later). An asset disposed of before 6 April 1985 could only be index-linked from the first anniversary of acquisition (or from March 1982 if later). This earlier indexation allowance could not increase or create a loss. The earlier allowance continued until 27 February 1986 in the cases of gilt-edged stocks and loan stocks.

3.1:3   Where the asset was acquired before 6 April 1965, the profit (or loss) prior to that date is eliminated either by using the market value at that date or by 'time apportionment' of the overall profit (or loss).

3.1:4   An individual is entitled to exempt gains up to a certain amount each year. For 1986/87 this amount is £6,300. Companies have no exempt amount. A trust's exempt amount is normally half that of an individual.

3.1:5   Where the disposal is by gift (and the gain is calculated by reference to market value) there may be an election to 'hold-over' the gain (See **3.2:2**).

3.1:6   The transfer of a business to a company can also provide an opportunity to elect for a 'hold-over'.

3.1:7   Where a chargeable disposal results in a loss, this may be used against gains of the same year and any excess carried forward against gains of later years. A loss brought forward cannot reduce the gains of any year below the amount of the annual exemption.

3.1:8   Gains on the sale of certain assets may be 'rolled over' by deducting them from the cost of new assets acquired within one year before and three years after the disposal. These are assets used in a trade and land compulsorily acquired.

3.1:9 A loan used by the borrower in his trade can give rise to an allowable loss by the lender. A loss by the guarantor of such a loan may also be claimed.

3.1:10 The gain on a 'part disposal' is based on the respective market values of what is disposed of and what is retained.

3.1:11 The grant of an option can be a part-disposal.

3.1:12 Stocks and shares are the subject of complicated rules regarding identification, pooling, rights and scrip issues, take-overs and other reorganisations.

3.1:13 Leases and lease premiums are also subject to special rules.

3.1:14 Gains accruing to a non-resident 'close' company can be apportioned to the shareholders.

3.1:15 The date of disposal is as follows:
(a) in a normal sale – the contract date;
(b) in a conditional sale – the date the condition is satisfied;
(c) in a vesting – the date the compensation is agreed or (if earlier) the date the authority enters the property.
   How the basic system is applied to trusts is described in **3.2.** to **3.10.** below.

3.2   THE GIFT INTO TRUST

3.2:1   By will on death

Where assets pass into trust under the will of a deceased person, they do so at the IHT value on the date of death. A disposal on death is exempt so that the estate pays no CGT. Nevertheless the trust acquires the assets at the IHT value and that value is the trust's 'cost' for the purpose of a future disposal.

3.2:2   By deed during settlor's lifetime

Where assets pass into trust by deed during the life of the settlor there is a disposal at market value — the settlor and his trustees are 'connected persons' under CGTA 1979, s 63(3). This market value may not be the value used for IHT. The settlor calculates his gain and either pays the CGT (if any) or if the gift is after 5 April 1981 elects to have the gain 'held-over' under FA 1981, s 78. He makes this election without the trustees having to join in. (Example **3.11:1**).

This election is not available after 17 March 1986 where the trust is double resident – see **6.3:7**.

3.2:3   An election to 'hold-over' results in the trust's acquisition value (the market value – Appendix II Note CGT 3) being reduced by the settlor's gain. This means of course that on a future disposal, the trust's gain is increased by the settlor's gain. In other words, the gain has been 'held-over' until the next time round (Example **3.11:2**).

3.2:4   It should be emphasised that the gift into trust during the life of the settlor is a chargeable disposal even if the settlor has an interest in the trust or is a trustee. And it is a disposal of the entire property even if the settlement is revocable – CGTA 1979, s 53.

3.2:5   Indexation on disposals up to 5 April 1985

The settlor may have been entitled to an indexation allowance at the time of his gift into trust if he had held the asset for more than 12 months and made his gift after March 1982. Where a 'hold-over' was claimed the reduced value at which the trust took the asset was effectively increased by the settlor's indexation allowance. This increase might later have been wholly or partly withdrawn if the trust had disposed of the asset at a loss. This was because indexation could not increase or create a loss.

The trust's own indexation allowance started 12 months after the gift into trust and was calculated on the market value at the date of the gift less the settlor's 'held-over' gain and plus the settlor's indexation allowance (See Example **3.11:3**). The normal rule applied to prevent this allowance increasing or creating a loss.

Thus this disposal at no profit/no loss was different from others – for example between spouses or between group companies – where the donee did not have to wait 12 months for an allowance.

3.2:6 Indexation on disposals after 5 April 1985

In calculating a gain on a disposal after 5 April 1985 there is no 12 month delay before indexation starts, and there is no longer a bar to indexation creating or increasing a loss. Thus the trust's indexation allowance starts from the date of gift (or March 1982 if later) and is based on the market value at the date of the gift less the settlor's 'held-over' gain and plus the settlor's indexation allowance. Where the gift into trust was before 31 March 1982 the allowance can be based on the market value at that date if that would be advantageous.

3.2:7 Inheritance tax on the gift

The gift into trust is a capital transfer for IHT and where the exemptions and zero-rate band have been used there will be a liability. This IHT can be treated as part of the cost of the gift into trust by deducting it from any gain on a subsequent disposal by the trust. This IHT cannot however increase or create a loss.

If the settlor dies within seven years of his gift the IHT may be increased and this increased amount can be substituted.

3.3 THE TRUST'S NORMAL GAINS

3.3:1 The trust will have gains in the ordinary course of managing its assets. One investment will be sold and another bought in the same way that an individual adjusts his portfolio. These gains are taxed in the same way as an individual's gains except that the annual exempt amount is reduced.

3.3:2 While an individual has an annual exemption of £6,300 (for 1986/87) the trust has £3,150. To prevent a settlor creating multiple exemptions the rules divide the exempt gain of £3,150 between the trusts created by the same settlor after 6 June 1978. If he has created five trusts each will have an annual exemption of £630 and this seems to be the minimum exempt amount even if more than five trusts have been set up. Also it would seem that husband and wife are treated as separate settlors for this purpose. Exemptions for prior years are shown in Appendix II Note CGT 4 (CGTA 1979, Sch 1, para 6).

The interaction of the annual exemption with losses brought forward is shown in Example **3.11:4**.

If the trust is for a mentally disabled person (**5.8**) or a person in receipt of attendance allowance, the annual exemption is as for an individual and not a trust.

3.3:3   A trust is not an individual and so it does not have a domicile. Thus the provision taxing a non-domiciled person's overseas gains on a remittance basis does not apply to trusts.

Similarly, the exemption of non-domiciled persons from tax on the gains of non-resident companies does not apply to trusts.

3.3:4   The provisions regarding transactions with connected persons apply to trusts. The persons connected with a trust are the settlor, any person connected with the settlor (Appendix II Note CGT 5), any partner of the trust, any company controlled by the trustees with their connected persons, any close company or non-resident 'close' company in which the trust is a participator and lastly any company controlled by such a company.

It seems that if the settlor is deceased, the persons listed in Appendix II Note CGT 5 will no longer be persons connected with the trust.

3.3:5   Where trustees do not pay tax within six months of the due date, the revenue can follow the asset or its proceeds into the hands of the beneficiaries (CGTA 1979, s 52 (4)).

3.3:6   The inspector may require any party to a settlement to provide information which he thinks he requires (CGTA 1979 Sch 1, para 5(3)).

3.3:7   Trusts are subject to the normal rules regarding indexation (see **3.2:5** and **3.2:6**), asssets held at 6 April 1965, roll-overs, losses, part disposals, options, leases etc.

3.4   A LIFE INTEREST ENDS ON DEATH

3.4:1   A life interest usually continues until the death of the life tenant and on that event the property may remain in trust or may leave the trust. It can remain in trust if someone else becomes entitled to the income or if the income becomes subject to the trustees' discretion.

3.4:2   Where the assets remain in trust there is a deemed disposal at market value but any gain is not chargeable (CGTA 1979, s 55

(1)). The same result will follow if the original beneficiary is still alive but a person to whom he sold his life interest dies (s 55 (3)).

The same result will follow if a beneficiary dies who was granted the income for some other person's life and that other person is still alive.

If the life interest which comes to an end was in a fraction of the property the deemed disposal is of that fraction only (Example **3.11:5**).

If the property was subject to a 'hold-over' election when it was transferred to the trust, that 'held-over' gain becomes taxable when the life interest in it ends on death. There can unfortunately be no new 'hold-over' election to defer the gain again because the asset is still in trust and there is no transferee to join in the election.

3.4:3 Where the assets cease to be in trust at the end of the life interest this will be because some beneficiary becomes absolutely entitled to them. See 'A beneficiary becomes absolutely entitled' (**3.5**).

A life interest ends otherwise than on death

3.4:4 On the other hand a life interest may end otherwise than on a death. This may happen if the interest is during some other person's minority or if the trustees exercise a right to appoint property away from the life tenant (Appendix II Note CGT 6). Again the property may remain in trust or may leave the trust.

3.4:5 Where the assets remain in trust some other beneficiary may become entitled to the income or the income may become subject to the trustees' discretion. Until 5 April 1982 the end of a life interest was a disposal for CGT but since that date there is no disposal while the assets remain in trust – FA 1982, s 84.

3.4:6 Where the assets cease to be in trust at the end of the life interest, see 'A beneficiary becomes absolutely entitled' (**3.5**).

Annuities

3.4:7 Where a trust creates an annuity and settled property is appropriated by the trustees as a fund out of which the annuity is payable and there is no right of recourse to other settled property or its income, then that annuity will be treated as a life interest in the appropriated property as if it were a separate settlement.

3.4:8   Where a trust creates an annuity not so charged on a separate fund it is not a life interest even though it is charged on the settled property or its income. Nevertheless on the death of the annuitant there is a disposal of a proportion of the trust property. This is the proportion which the annuity bears to the total settlement income in the year before the death.

3.5   A BENEFICIARY BECOMES ABSOLUTELY ENTITLED

3.5:1   Where a beneficiary takes an asset on the death of the life tenant (or of some other person) there is a disposal at market value but no liability to CGT. Thus the beneficiary takes the asset at market value – CGTA 1979, s 54 (1).

If the asset was subject to a 'hold-over' election when it was transferred to the trust, that 'held-over' gain becomes taxable when the beneficiary becomes absolutely entitled (Example **3.11:6**). There can however be a new 'hold-over' election by the trustees and the beneficiary jointly – FA 1982, s 82 (Appendix II Note CGT 7).

3.5:2   On the other hand the beneficiary may become absolutely entitled on an occasion other than death, for example, when he attains a certain age, or when the trustees exercise discretion in his favour. Again there is a disposal at market value (CGTA 1979, s 54 (1)) but in this case CGT is payable. This disposal at market value also applies if the beneficiary would have become absolutely entitled but for being an infant or under some other disability.

3.5:3   If the disposal is after 5 April 1982 the trustees and the beneficiary can jointly elect for a 'hold-over'. This results in the beneficiary's 'cost' (the market value) being reduced by the trust's gain and the beneficiary's future gain being increased by the same amount. (Example **3.11:7**).

This 'hold-over' is not available if the beneficiary is not resident in the UK (Appendix II Note CGT 7).

3.5:4   The indexation position is the same as when there is hold-over on a gift into trust. That is the trust's cost is increased by the trust's indexation allowance and this increased cost attracts the beneficiary's allowance from the date on which he becomes entitled, or from 12 months thereafter if his disposal is before 6 April 1985.

3.5:5   If the value of the asset at the date the beneficiary takes it results in a loss the trust may be able to set this against other gains.

If the trust cannot claim the capital loss it may be carried forward by the beneficiary who takes that asset – CGTA 1979, s 54 (2). See **7.3:5.**

As well as losses forward the beneficiary can increase his acquisition value by any costs of transfer incurred by himself or by the trustees.

3.6 PROPERTY REVERTS TO THE SETTLOR

Where an asset reverts from the trust to the settlor it does so on a no profit/no loss basis. In other words the settlor takes the asset at the trust's base value.

3.7 A LIFE INTEREST BEGINS

This may happen when a beneficiary attains a certain age – for example, in an accumulation and maintenance trust. Such occasions are not disposals for CGT purposes.

3.8 A BENEFICIARY DISPOSES OF HIS INTEREST

3.8:1 It is possible for a beneficiary to sell his interest in a trust or to give it away. It may be a present right to receive income or it may be a future right to income or capital. In no case is this a disposal for CGT by the trust. In most cases it is not a taxable disposal for CGT by the beneficiary because this would give rise to an element of double taxation. The exception is set out in the next paragraph (**3.8:2**).

The beneficiary is treated as disposing of his interest on becoming absolutely entitled to the assets but again this is an exempt disposal subject to **3.8:2**.

3.8:2 The exception is where the interest has been purchased (Appendix II Note CGT 8). Thus the original beneficiary, Mr A may fall on hard times and sell his interest to Mr B. If Mr B subsequently sells the interest, that is a disposal for CGT (Appendix II Note CGT 9).

3.9   DWELLING OCCUPIED BY BENEFICIARY

3.9:1   Where a dwelling house owned by the trust is occupied by a beneficiary who is entitled to do so under the terms of the trust as his sole or main residence, any gain on disposal by the trust is exempt from CGT. There is apportionment in the usual way if it was not so occupied during the whole period of ownership.

3.9:2   In a discretionary trust the conditions are satisfied if the beneficiary's occupation is with the permission of the trustees under the terms of the trust – *Sansom v Peay* [1976] STC 494. Where however this arrangement has any permanence, the Revenue may regard it as an 'interest in possession' for IHT.

3.9:3   If a beneficiary occupies two such dwelling houses, he and the trustees must make a joint election as to which is his main residence (CGTA 1979, s 104).

3.10   A BENEFICIARY RETIRES

3.10:1   Introduction

A beneficiary may retire from his family company or from his business and qualify for retirement relief for CGT purposes but he cannot get it if the shares or the business premises, for example, are not owned by him but by a trust. Provision is therefore made for the trust to get the relief where the 'qualifying period' ends after 5 April 1985.

A qualifying period is one of at least one year ending within one year of the disposal and the conditions below have to be observed during this period.

3.10:2   Retirement relief on disposal of shares

Where a trust disposes of shares in a trading company or in the holding company of a trading group there may be an entitlement to retirement relief. The conditions which have to be satisfied during the qualifying period are:

(a) A beneficiary must have had an interest in possession (not for a fixed time) in the shares.

(b) The company must have been the beneficiary's family company.

(c) The beneficiary must have been a full-time working director of the company or of a company in the group.
(d) He must have ceased to be such a director within one year before disposal. The Revenue may extend this time limit.
(e) He must have reached 60 years of age when he ceased to be such a director or his retirement must have been due to ill-health.

3.10:3 Retirement relief on disposal of business asset

Similarly a trust may be entitled to retirement relief on the disposal of an asset used in a business. The same conditions suitably adapted apply during the qualifying period as follows:
(a) The beneficiary must have had an interest in possession (not for a fixed term) in the asset.
(b) The asset must have been used in the business.
(c) The beneficiary must have carried on the business alone or in partnership.
(d) He must have ceased to carry on the business within one year before the disposal. The Revenue may extend this time limit.
(e) He must have reached 60 years of age when he ceased to carry on the trade or his retirement must have been due to ill-health.

3.11   CAPITAL GAINS TAX EXAMPLES

3.11:1   Example CGT 1 (see 3.2:2)

	£
Market value of asset gifted into trust in April 1982	5,000
Cost of asset to the settlor in April 1962	1,470
Total gain	3,530
Fraction (on time basis) falling after April 1965 $\dfrac{17 \text{ years}}{20 \text{ years}}$	£3,000

(The calculation is made by reference to 6 April 1965 in months and fractions of months)
Where the gift into trust was after 5 April 1981 the settlor can elect for a 'hold-over' of this gain (Example **3.11:2**)

3.11:2   Example CGT 2 (see 3.2:3)

	£	£
Sale by the trust in June 1986 of the asset acquired in Example **3.11:1**		10,000
Market value when acquired in 1982	5,000	
Less settlor's 'held-over' gain	3,000	
	2,000	
Add indexation from April 1982	350	
IHT paid on gift into trust in April 1982	—	
		2,350
Gain by the trust		7,650
Other gains in the same fiscal year		3,450
		11,100
Annual exemption		3,150
Taxable gains		7,950
CGT @ 30%		2,385

Note As the trust's disposal was after 5 April 1985 there is no 12 month delay before indexation allowance operates.

3.11:3 Example CGT 3 (see 3.2:5)

	£
Cost to the settlor in December 1982	4,000
Market value on gift into trust in March 1985	6,000
Settlor's gross gain	2,000
Less indexation allowance from December 1983 to March 1985	250
Net gain	1,750

Note As the settlor's disposal was before 6 April 1985 there is a delay of 12 months before the indexation allowance operates.

Trust acquisition value in March 1985

	£
Market value at date of gift	6,000
Less settlor's held-over gain	1,750
(equivalent to settlor's cost £4,000 plus settlor's indexation allowance £250)	4,250
Sale by trust in December 1987	7,000
Trust's gross gain	2,750
Less trust's indexation allowance (based on £4,250) from March 1985 to December 1987	500
Trust net gain	2,250

Note As the trust's disposal is after 5 April 1985 there is no 12 months delay and indexation operates from the acquisition date

3.11:4 Example CGT 4 (see 3.3:2)

	£
Gains by the trust in 1986/87	4,500
Annual exemption in 1986/87	3,150
	1,350
Losses brought forward from 1985/86	2,000
Losses carried forward to 1987/88	650

3.11:5   **Example CGT 5** (see **3.4:2**)

	£	Half in which A's life interest ends £	Half in which B's life interest continues £
Asset purchased by the trust in October 1984	8,000	4,000	4,000
Market value on death of A in December 1986 (this gain is tax-free)	10,000	5,000	
Sale of asset in April 1988	12,000	6,000	6,000
Gain		1,000	2,000
Indexation of £5,000 from December 1986 to April 1988		400	
Indexation of £4,000 from October 1984 to April 1988			800
		600	1,200
Taxable gain		£1,800	

Note Indexation of A's half share from October 1984 to December 1986 is irrelevant because the gain is tax-free on his death.

3.11:6   **Example CGT 6** (see **3.5:1**)

	£
Trustee's acquisition value in March 1985 per Example **3.11:3**	6,000
Less settlor's held-over gain	1,750
	4,250
Market value in December 1987 when beneficiary becomes absolutely entitled on death of life tenant	7,000
	2,750
Trust's indexation allowance (based on £4,250) from March 1985 to December 1987	500
	2,250
Trust's gain exempt on a death	500
Settlor's held-over gain now taxable	1,750
	2,250

It is believed that this taxable gain can be held-over again, but it is not certain.

3.11:7   Example CGT 7 (see 3.5:3)

	£
Asset purchased by the trust in October 1981	9,000
Market value when beneficiary becomes absolutely entitled on becoming 21 in March 1987	16,000
	7,000
Trust's indexation allowance from March 1982 (earliest date for indexation) to March 1987 based on market value at March 1982 – £10,000	3,000
Trust's gain which is taxable (not on a death) but available for hold-over	4,000

Beneficiary's cost:

	£
Market value	16,000
Less held-over gain	4,000
	12,000

The beneficiary's own indexation allowance on a future disposal is based on £12,000.

Chapter 4   Inheritance Tax
(Formerly Capital Transfer Tax)

4.1   INTRODUCTION

4.1:1   The former system

(a) From 1974 until 1981 CTT was charged on capital transfers during the life of the taxpayer (gifts) on an accumulation basis. That is to say the larger the accumulated total of gifts after 26 March 1974 the higher the rate of CTT on the latest gifts. There was a final accumulation of the capital passing on the death of the taxpayer with the lifetime transfers since 27 March 1974. There were two scales of rates to be used – a lower scale for lifetime transfers and a higher scale on death. A gift within three years of death was reassessed on the higher scale.

(b) From 10 March 1981 to 17 March 1986 the period of accumulation was reduced to ten years both for gifts and deaths between those dates. That is to say a gift dropped out of the calculation after ten years. There were still two scales of rates and a gift within three years of death was still reassessed on the higher scale.

4.1:2   The present system

For deaths after 17 March 1986 the property passing is added to the gifts of the previous seven years (instead of ten) and the total is taxed on the only scale of rates. These rates are unchanged from the previous death scale, although the bands are index-linked.

The value of the estate on death is the top slice of the accumulation.

The gifts within seven years of death form the lowest slice of the charge on death and this tax on lifetime gifts at death rates is tapered where the donor survives his gift by more than three years.

If he survives three years 80% of the tax is payable

,,	,,	4	,,	60%	,,	,,
,,	,,	5	,,	40%	,,	,,
,,	,,	6	,,	80%	,,	,,
,,	,,	7	,,	none	,,	,,

Where a lifetime gift is the subject of a charge on death, the tax falls on the donee but with recourse to the estate.

4.1:3   Where a gift is made with reservation – that is to say it is not enjoyed by the recipient to the entire exclusion of the donor – the charge on death is calculated as if the gift were made when the reservation was released or the enjoyment ceased (if later). In a case where the reservation is not released the gifted property is treated as passing on death at its then value.

The gift of a house where the donor continues to live in it would come under this rule. So would a gift into a discretionary (but not a fixed interest) trust of which the settlor is a beneficiary.

4.1:4 Where a debt due by the deceased at his death has not been incurred for full consideration and for the deceased's own use or benefit, or where the creditor had received gifts from the deceased, the debt will not be allowed in reduction of the estate. This would apply where the settlor has received loans from his trust.

Lifetime gifts

4.1:5 Lifetime gifts to individuals after 17 March 1986 are not liable to tax at the time of gift although they may attract tax if the donor dies within seven years. Such a gift is a potentially exempt transfer (PET).

4.1:6 Other lifetime gifts (ie gifts into trust or gifts involving companies) continue to be liable with a seven year accumulation period (instead of ten). These rates are half the death rates as before although no separate scale is provided. See **4.2:1** for details of the transfers cumulated.

This lifetime charge applies even if the gift is made with reservation and would still form part of the settlor's estate for a charge on death. This would happen if, for example, the settlor were a beneficiary of a discretionary (but not a fixed interest) trust that he had created.

4.1:7 Where a lifetime gift is subject to a lifetime charge it may later be subject to a death charge where 1. the settlor dies within seven years, or 2. the gift is made with reservation and the reservation is not released more than seven years before death. In these circumstances the lifetime charge is allowed as a credit against the death charge. Due to tapering relief the death charge may be smaller, and in that case the credit is abated.

4.1:8 Transitional provisions

(a) Where a lifetime gift made before 18 March 1986 becomes liable on a subsequent death, no more tax is payable than would have been the case had the former system continued.

(b) The new rules about gifts with reservation do not apply to gifts made before 18 March 1986.
(c) The new rules about debts not deductible on death do not apply to debts incurred before 18 March 1986.

4.1:9 Exemptions

Certain exemptions apply to events before 18 March 1986 as well as to later events. They apply to lifetime gifts which are chargeable at the time of the gift and also to PETS that become chargeable on a death within seven years.

(a) *During lifetime*
   Gifts which are normal expenditure out of income.
   The first £3,000 of capital gifts each year.
   All gifts not exceeding £250 each.
   Wedding gifts depending on the family relationship (See **5.3:4**).
   Dispositions for the maintenance of a spouse, a child or a dependant relative.

(b) *During lifetime and on death*
   Transfers to a spouse domiciled in the UK.
   Transfers to a charity, a political party or certain other bodies.
   Transfers allowed in computing business profits.
   Transfers of excluded property (see Appendix III Note IHT 1).
   Transfers not intended to convey any gratuitous benefit.

4.1:10 Reliefs

30% or 50% of business property.
30% or 50% of certain shares.
30% or 50% of agricultural property.
Tapering for quick succession.
Deferral for growing timber.

4.1:11 Loss to the donor

The original idea of CTT was to assess eventually the taxpayer's whole estate and therefore each capital transfer is not the amount received by the donee but the reduction in the estate of the donor.

This can be illustrated by a gift of shares in a company which reduces the donor's holding from 55% to 45% of the ordinary capital. The loss is not just the 10% received by the donee but the loss of control of the company suffered by the donor.

The other common illustration is where the tax is borne by the donor. The loss to his estate is the gift plus the tax ie the gift has to be 'grossed up'. This 'grossing up' will apply on a lifetime gift into trust where the settlor bears the tax, but not to all transfers by the trust (See Appendix III Note IHT 14). By contrast, CGT paid by the donor is ignored.

4.2 THE GIFT INTO TRUST

4.2:1 The transfer of capital by the settlor into his trust comes under the foregoing system. Where the trust is formed by deed during the life of settlor there is no exemption as there would be if the gift were to an individual after 17 March 1986. The loss to his estate is measured as described and any exemption deducted. The resulting taxable amount is added to the taxable transfers (excluding PETS) of the previous seven years (ten years if the gift were before 18 March 1986) and the tax is calculated at half the scale of rates depending on whether the tax is to be paid by the trust (Example **4.10:1**) or by the settlor (Example **4.10:2**). In the latter case of course the gift has to be 'grossed up'. The taxable transfers of the previous seven years will include gifts into trust, gifts involving companies and the ending of any interest in possession (**4.3:5**).

4.2:2 There are a few trusts where diffferent rules apply to the settlor's gift. If it is a marriage settlement by a parent of one of the parties there is an exemption of £5,000 in addition to the normal annual £3,000. If it is, for example, an employees' trust the whole gift may be exempt. If it is an accumulation and maintenance trust (**5.1**) or a trust for the disabled (**5.8**) the gift is treated as one to an individual if it is made after 17 March 1986 (ie it is a PET).

4.2:3 A gift into a discretionary trust in which the settlor is a beneficiary is a gift with reservation (**4.1:3**). Where the settlor's spouse is a beneficiary this may not be a reserved benefit. A gift into a fixed interest trust in which the settlor or his spouse has an interest in possession is not a gift with reservation – the part in which he or she has an interest in possession is not a transfer at all.

4.2:4 The gift into trust may on the other hand be by will on the death of the settlor and in this case there are three differences:
(a) We use the full scale rates – (rather than half).
(b) There is no 'grossing up'. The testator cannot leave more than he has.

(c) The calculation involves the whole estate, not just the assets going into trust.
See Example **4.10:3**.

4.3   THE TRUST'S OWN LIABILITY

4.3:1   Introduction

The foregoing relates to the settlor's tax – whether borne by him or by the trust – and we must now consider the trust's own liability.

As the exemption of lifetime gifts to individuals does not apply to gifts into trust, so it does not apply to the various events in the life of the trust itself – they are in most cases liable to tax. But IHT was designed to tax the passing on of an individual's wealth, and there are many problems in trying to apply the system to trusts.

Probably the best introduction to the liability of trusts to IHT is to consider these problems in turn.

4.3:2   Interest in possession

Problem A
A trust is not an individual and so the concept of an individual's 'transfers' in the previous seven years presents a difficulty and a new principle has to be introduced.

This new rule deals with the trust assets in the simplest possible way by asking us to pretend that they are owned by the person entitled to the income from them. In IHT language there is an 'interest in possession' (See Appendix III Note IHT 2).

4.3:3   End of 'interest in possession' on death

This 'interest in possession' may come to an end on the death of the person entitled to the income and in these circumstances we have to increase his personal estate by the market value of the trust assets from which he was entitled to the income. We then calculate the tax on this increased estate by taking account of both the taxable transfers and the PETS by the late life tenant, during the last seven years of his life. The lifetime gifts are the lowest slice and the personal estate plus the trust assets (of which the deceased was the tenant) form the top slice (Example **4.10:4**).

4.3:4 Apportionment of IHT

Problem B
This gives rise to the second problem because some of the assets
charged are available to the executors of the late life tenant for the
payment of tax and some are not (being either in the trust or having
been gifted prior to death).

So we are required to apportion the tax on the top slice rateably
between the personal assets and the trust assets. The former portion
is payable out of the personal assets of the late life tenant and latter
portion out of the trust assets in which he had an 'interest in possession'. The tax on the lowest slice (less credit for any tax at the time
of the gift) is payable in the first instance by the donees but with
recourse to the estate of the deceased (Example **4.10:4**).

4.3:5 End of 'interest in possession' during life

Problem C
An 'interest in possession' will not always come to an end on the death
of the person entitled to it – it may end during his lifetime. This may
happen if the terms of the trust have given him his interest for the
lifetime of someone else or until someone else comes of age or until
he re-marries or some other period which happens to end during his
lifetime. It will also happen if he renounces or if the trustees appoint
it away from him.

In these circumstances we must follow the same basic rule – we must
calculate the tax on the trust assets as if they had been transferred
by the person who ceased to be entitled to the income from them
and for this purpose we must take into account his chargeable transfers during the previous seven years (ten years if the interest ended
before 18 March 1986). There are of course four differences from
the position where the 'interest in possession' ends on the death of
the 'tenant'. These differences are:
(a) The personal assets of the 'tenant' are not being transferred and
    need not be counted.
(b) The 'tenant' is still alive and we will use half the rates in the table.
(c) The resulting tax relates only to the trust assets and does not
    need to be apportioned. It is all payable by the trust. (Example
    4.10:5).
(d) Gifts by the tenant to individuals are not taken into account if
    the interest ceases after 17 March 1986.

It might be thought that the surrender of a life interest by one individual in favour of another individual should be a PET. But it is not, it is taxable.

An individual's exemptions and reliefs are available if the tenant elects to make them so (IHTA 1984, s 57). This will cover the annual exemption and the exemption for gifts in consideration of marriage.

4.3:6   End of an 'interest in possession' on reversion to settlor

Where assets which have been the subject of a fixed interest revert to the settlor the transfer is exempt. The exemption will also apply to a reversion to the settlor's spouse within two years of the settlor's death.

4.3:7   End of an 'interest in possession' on sale

Where a life tenant sells his interest he will expect to receive less than the market value of the underlying assets. This difference is a chargeable transfer.

4.3:8   End of an 'interest in possession' on becoming an absolute interest

Problem D
The person entitled to the income from the assets may become entitled to the assets themselves. This may happen if the remainderman were to predecease the life tenant and the latter were to take his place.

For the purpose of IHT we are asked to deal with interests in possession by pretending that the tenant is the absolute owner and so when this in fact happens there are no tax consequences. The assets are part of his estate until he gifts them or dies.

4.3:9   End of an 'interest in expectancy' (Appendix III Note IHT 3)

Problem E
A person may be in line to receive a future interest on the death of another (normally the life tenant) or on some other occasion. He may decide to pass this future interest on to his children.

Again, the rule is that the transfer of capital takes place when the life interest ends. Thus we can ignore the fact that there has been a change in the identity of the person to receive the interest in expectancy.

If the full value of the assets is to be regarded as part of the life tenant's estate, there is no part of that value left to attach to the remainder. This useful rule is subject to three exceptions:

(a) Where the future interest has been acquired for money or money's worth.
(b) Where the settlor or his spouse is or was beneficially entitled to the future interest. This is because the value of the settlor's gift into trust was reduced by the value of the interest he retained.
(c) Where the future interest will arise on the termination of a lease which is treated as a settlement.

4.3:10 Transactions treated as reducing an 'interest in possession'

The trustees (Appendix III Note IHT 4) may enter into a transaction with the beneficiaries, or potential beneficiaries the result of which is to depreciate the value of trust property below what it would otherwise have been. In these circumstances the appropriate fraction of any interests in possession are treated as coming to an end with the resultant charge to IHT – IHTA 1984, s 52 (3). This can be avoided if it is shown that there was no gratuitous intent – IHTA 1984, s 10.

4.3:11 Transfers by close company

Where the trust is a participator in a close company a transfer of value by the company may be apportioned between the shareholders including the trust. The part apportioned to the trust is then apportioned to interests in possession and that part of each interest in possession is treated as having ended. This may give rise to a tax liability dependent on the life tenant's position.

If, however, the transfer by the company results in an increase in the values of trust property, this has to be taken into account.

4.4   TRUST ASSETS WITHOUT 'INTEREST IN POSSESSION'

4.4:1   Introduction

This relatively simple system breaks down in its turn if there are trust assets from which no one is entitled to the income. They are assets without an 'interest in possession'.

The income from such assets does not disappear just because no one is entitled to it, and of course it cannot remain 'in limbo', so the normal position is that the trustees are instructed by the trust deed to accumulate it, or are given discretion as to what to do with it. Where all the income of a trust is subject to such provisions the trust is described as 'discretionary' and such a trust is liable to tax as described below. But it is important to recognise that a trust may not be entirely discretionary. The trust deed may give an 'interest in possession' in some assets and not in others. Thus the distinction is not between discretionary trusts and other trusts but between the different assets to be charged. The distinction in other words is according to whether some person has or has not the immediate right to the income from that asset.

Such assets are treated as transferred when they cease to be assets without an interest in possession – that is when they cease to be relevant property (Appendix III Note IHT 5) such occasions are listed in Appendix III Note IHT 6.

The liability on these occasions can be complicated but it has two great advantages – it is never calculated at death rates and the assets are never aggregated with the estate of the settlor or a beneficiary. The calculation depends on whether the trust was formed before or after the advent of CTT in 1974.

4.5   TRUST ASSETS WITHOUT 'INTEREST IN POSSESSION' – TRUST FORMED PRE 27 MARCH 1974

4.5:1   Introduction

Problem F
Where these assets are to be treated as transferred there is no transferor in the ordinary IHT terminology. Neither is there any 'tenant' whose personal tax position can be used.

Thus a new system comes into operation which treats the trust as a live person in its own right with its own scale of rates (divorced from the rates of any beneficiary) but with no annual exemptions.

4.5:2   The periodic charge

Problem G
The next problem with these assets arises from the fact that there is

no 'tenant' to give up his rights (on death or during his lifetime). Thus there may not be a 'transfer' at all.

The IHT regime tackles this problem by making a 'periodic charge' every ten years at 30% of the full tax. The logic behind this seems to be that if capital will normally pass to the next generation every 30 years or so and suffer 100% of the normal tax, then 30% every ten years is about the same burden – IHTA 1984, ss 66 and 67.

The first periodic charge is levied on the tenth anniversary (or multiple of ten) of the settlement falling after 31 March 1983 and is calculated on a transfer equal to the market value of the relevant property in the trust at that date. The calculation is at lifetime rates taking into account the 'transfers' (Appendix III Note IHT 6) by the trust in the previous ten years. The resulting tax is then reduced to 30% of its full amount (Example **4.10:6**). This is then expressed as an effective rate for future use.

4.5:3   Transfers between periodic charges

Problem H
This in its turn gives rise to another problem because in practice there will be capital transfers which also have to be charged, and a method of avoiding a double charge has to be devised.

The solution adopted is to regard the periodic charge as accruing from quarter to quarter over the ten years. Thus when there is a transfer the capital involved bears the number of complete quarters accrued since the last periodic charge. The rate on which the calculation is based is the 'effective rate' of the last periodic charge (Example **4.10:7**) IHTA 1984, s 68. It follows that there is no tax on a 'transfer' made within three months after a periodic charge.

4.5:4   Transfer before first periodic charge

Problem I
This leads to a further problem where the transfer takes place before the first periodic charge.

Where the trust was formed before 1974 the first periodic charge (which can't fall before 1 April 1983) may be made many years after the settlement date, and the charge on assets transferred before then simply consists of the same 30% of normal IHT which will be charged on the remaining assets when the time for the periodic charge comes (Example **4.10:8**).

4.5:5   Additional relevant property

Problem J
Then there is the problem caused by assets being added to the trust between periodic charges, or becoming relevant property between periodic charges.

We have seen under Problem H that where an asset leaves the trust between periodic charges the CTT for the number of accrued quarters is charged. Where an asset is added to a trust or becomes relevant property the same principle is applied by reducing the charge (on the next ten year anniversary) by the number of completed quarters between the previous ten year anniversary and the date the asset was added (Example **4.10:9**).

Adding property to an existing trust is not advisable in most cases – see Problem L (**4.5:7**) below.

4.5:6   Transfer after addition

Problem K
There may be a transfer after the asset has been added (or becomes relevant property) and before the next periodic charge.

In these circumstances the effective rate of the last periodic charge has to be recalculated as if the added property had been relevant property at that time (Example **4.10:10**).

4.5:7   Anti-avoidance after addition

Problem L
A settlor (Appendix III Note IHT 7) might seek to use the advantage of a pre-1974 trust by adding property to it rather than forming a new post-1974 trust.

This is countered by providing that the 'snowball' used in calculating the periodic or exit charges shall include not only the transfers by the trust in the previous ten years but also the taxable transfers by the settlor in the seven years preceding the transfer which increased the value of the trust (ten years if the transfer was after 8 March 1982 and before 18 March 1986). We exclude transfers made on that day and any other items already included in the calculation (Example **4.10:11**).

4.5:8 Property again becoming relevant

Problem M
It is possible for property to cease to be relevant and to bear an exit charge, and later to become relevant again (eg on the death of a life tenant). Thus such property could be counted twice – once as relevant property at the date of a periodic charge and once in the transfers of the previous ten years.

Where this happens – ie where the exit charge was in the previous ten years – the 'snowball' is reduced by whichever of the two values is lower (Example **4.10:12**).

4.6 TRUSTS ASSETS WITHOUT 'INTEREST IN POSSESSION' – TRUST FORMED AFTER 26 MARCH 1974

4.6:1 Distinguished from older trusts

Problem N
The next problem arises out of the fact that the trusts we have been considering were set up before the advent of CTT in 1974 and so the settlor did not know what he was letting his trustees in for. Others were set up since 1974 and so the settlor could try to take steps to mitigate the trustees' liability.

This is countered by requiring us to calculate the IHT in the latter case by taking into account the settlor's taxable transfers in the seven years prior to the settlement (ten years if the charge was before 18 March 1986) as well as the trust's own transfers in the ten years prior to the periodic charge.

The periodic charge (IHTA 1984, s 64) is arrived at (as with the pre-CTT trusts) by valuing the relevant property at the date of the charge, applying half the scale rates and reducing the resultant tax to 30% of its full amount (Example **4.10:13**). This is then expressed as an effective rate for future use.

4.6:2   Non-relevant property

Problem O
The settlor's taxable transfers in the seven or ten years prior to the settlement date are the same transfers used in calculating his IHT liability when he transferred assets into the settlement and so do not include transfers on that date.

To correct this we are required to include the other assets put into the trust – that is assets in which there is an interest in possession (assets which are not relevant property) provided they had not otherwise been charged (Example **4.10:13**). This gives rise to a strong case for not having relevant and non-relevant property in the same trust.

4.6:3   Property which has changed class

Problem P
The settlor might have put into the trust assets which subsequently became 'relevant property' and so would be liable to the periodic charge (etc). He also may have put into the trust assets which were then 'relevant property' but later ceased to be so and were subject to an exit charge. In both cases double taxation would arise.

To overcome this we do not have to take account of all the other assets settled but only assets in the trust at the date of the charge which were not then relevant property and had never been relevant property. The value however is still to be the value when they were settled. It should be emphasised that such assets are not charged but merely used in arriving at the effective rate of charge (Example **4.10:13**).

4.6:4   Related trusts

Problem Q
This would leave it open to the settlor to reduce the rate of charge by putting some of the assets into another trust on the same day (if he did it on a previous day it would be included in his 'snowball').

So we are required to take into account the value of assets put into other trusts formed on the same day (Related trusts – Appendix III Note IHT 8). Again the value taken is that when they were settled. As with non-relevant property, the assets are not charged but merely used in arriving at the effective rate of charge (Example **4.10:13**).

4.6:5 The five elements in the calculation

Thus there is a procedure to be followed in calculating a charge which can be quite complicated.

1 The transfer

	Value
(a) The part charged is the relevant property at the date of the periodic charge	Value at the date of charge
(b) The part not charged but used in calculating the rate of charge is:	
(1) the rest of the trust property at the date of the periodic charge, provided it had never been relevant property	Value immediately after settlement
(2) Property put into a related trust	

2 The snowball

(a) The 'transfers' by the trust in the ten years preceding the periodic charge	Values at dates of transfers
(b) The taxable transfers by the settlor in the seven (or ten) years prior to the settlement	

    Note   Excluded property (Appendix III Note IHT 1) does not enter the calculation.

4.6:6 Transfer between periodic charges

> *Problem R*
> This is a 'transfer' between periodic charges (referred to in connection with a pre-1974 trust in Problem H) which would give rise to double taxation.

The solution is to regard the periodic charge as accruing from quarter to quarter over the ten years. Thus when there is a transfer the capital involved bears the number of quarters since the last periodic charge. The rate on which the calculation is based is the 'effective' rate of the last periodic charge (Example **4.10:14**). It follows that there is no tax on a 'transfer' within three months after a periodic charge.

The effective rate of the last periodic charge will have to be recalculated in the following circumstances:

(a) Where a new scale of rates has come into force.
(b) Where the settlor has died and a PET has become taxable. (This may happen retrospectively).
(c) Where the periodic charge was before 18 March 1986 and the 'transfer' after 17 March 1986. In this case there will be a change from ten years transfers to seven years taxable transfers.

4.6:7   Transfer before first periodic charge

Problem S
This arises where the transfer is before the first periodic charge so that we can't count the quarters since the periodic charge.

For a post-1974 trust the first periodic charge is ten years after the settlement date and so the accruing quarters simply count from the settlement date (Example **4.10:15**). The rate on which the calculation is based is 30% of the effective rate charged on a notional transfer at the rates in force at the date of charge but using the values at the date of settlement. The rate thus calculated is applied to the property ceasing to be relevant at its value at that time. It follows that there is no tax on a 'transfer' within three months of the settlement date. It also follows that where the settlor has not exceeded his zero-rate band on his gift into trust, there is normally no tax on 'transfer' before the first periodic charge. However, such a liability can arise as shown in Example **4.10:16**. It can also arise where the settlor has died and a PET has become taxable.

4.6:8   Additional relevant property

Problem T
This is caused by assets being added to the trust or becoming relevant property between periodic charges.

The solution is to reduce the next periodic charge by the number of complete quarters between the previous periodic charge and the date the asset was added (Example **4.10:17**).

4.6:9 Transfer after addition

Problem U
There may be a transfer after the asset has been added (or become relevant property) and before the next periodic charge.

In these circumstances the effective rate of the last periodic charge has to be re-calculated as if the added property had been relevant property at that time (Example **4.10:18**).

4.6:10 Anti-avoidance after addition

Problem V
A settlor might initially put a small amount of property into the trust or do it at a time when his 'snowball' was at a minimum. He might later add the main property when his 'snowball' was greater.

This is countered by providing that if the transfer which increases the value of the trust is after 8 March 1982 then the transfers by the settlor in the seven (or ten) years preceding the addition can be substituted (if they are greater) for his transfers in the seven (or ten) years preceding the original settlement, in the next calculation of a charge (IHTA 1984, s 67). As before, transfers on the same day as the transfer into trust are ignored, as are any other items already included in the calculation (Example **4.10:19**).

In view of this provision (and of the advantages of separate smaller trusts (Example **4.10:20**)) it is usually inadvisable to add property to an existing trust.

4.6:11 Property again becoming relevant

Problem W
It is possible for property to cease to be relevant and to bear an exit charge, and later to become relevant again (for example, on the death of a life tenant). Thus such property could be counted twice.

Where this happens – ie where the exit charge was in the previous ten years – the 'snowball' is reduced by whichever of the two values is lower (Example **4.10:21**).

There follows a summary of the provisions explained above (**4.7**) and details of the application of the exemptions and reliefs to trusts (**4.8**).

4.7   SUMMARY OF INHERITANCE TAX ON TRUSTS

Assuming that the settlor does not add any property to the trust after 8 March 1982 (or increase the value of the trust in any other way) and assuming that the occasion of charge is after 17 March 1986, the provisions can be summarised as follows:

4.7:1   Assets with a tenant

(a) Where an interest in possession ceases on the death of the tenant we treat the assets in which the interest ceases as transferred with the tenant's personal estate. We take account of the tenant's transfers during the last seven years of his life as the lowest slice and apportion the tax on the top slice rateably between the trust assets and his personal estate.

(b) Where an interest in possession ceases during the life of the tenant the tax is calculated as if the termination were a taxable lifetime transfer by the tenant of the assets in which the interest ceases (again taking account of his taxable transfers in the previous seven years).

(c) An interest in possession may partially cease and that is a transfer of that part. The tenant may have been entitled to a fractional part of the income and again the cessation is of that fraction of the capital assets.

(d) Where the interest is in a fixed amount of income (an annuity) the capital is divided between the interests according to certain rates of return.

(e) In the case of a lease for life at a nominal rent, the tenant is treated as having an interest in possession to the extent of the difference between the consideration he pays and the full market consideration.

(f) A transaction between the trustees and a beneficiary (or potential beneficiary) which reduces the value of trust assets, will give rise to a tax charge.

(g) A transfer of a reversionary interest will not give rise to a charge (except as set out in Appendix III Note IHT 3).

4.7:2   Assets without a tenant

(Trust formed before 27 March 1974)
(a) On each tenth anniversary of the formation of the trust falling after 31 March 1983 (Appendix III Note IHT 9) tax is calculated

as if the relevant property was being transferred by a live individual not entitled to annual exemptions. The periodic charge is 30% of this amount. There is no 'grossing up'. The 'snowball' is the total value of assets ceasing to be relevant property in the previous ten years.

(b) Where an asset ceases to be relevant property before the first periodic charge the same calculation is made and the resultant effective rate is applied to the market value of the asset 'transferred'.

(c) Where an asset becomes relevant property between periodic charges the tax on that asset at the next ten year anniversary is reduced by the number of completed quarters (out of 40) that the asset has not been in the trust, or has not been relevant property.

(d) Where an asset ceases to be relevant property between periodic charges it is subject to an exit charge at the effective rate of the previous periodic charge recalculated on the current scale and reduced to the number of completed quarters (out of 40) since that date.

4.7:3   Assets without a tenant

(Trust formed after 26 March 1974)

(a) On each tenth anniversary IHT is charged as in **4.7:2** (a) above except that the 'snowball' includes not only the 'transfers' by the trust in the previous ten years but also the taxable transfers by the settlor in the seven years prior to the settlement. The 'transfers' used in finding the effective rate of tax include not only the relevant property in the trust at the tenth anniversary (at its then market value) but also trust assets which were never relevant property and assets in related trusts both valued when they were settled. When 30% of the effective rate is thus calculated, it is applied only to the relevant property at the anniversary date.

(b) Where an asset ceases to be relevant property before the first periodic charge the same calculation is made but the remaining relevant property is also at the value when settled. The resultant effective rate is reduced to the number of completed quarters (out of 40) since the formation of the trust. This rate is then applied to the current market value of the 'transfer'.

(c) Where an asset becomes relevant property between periodic charges the treatment at the next periodic charge is as in **4.7:2** (c) above.

(d) Where an asset ceases to be relevant property between periodic charges it is taxed as in **4.7:2** (d) above. The previous periodic charge may require to be recalculated (1) if there is a new scale of rates (2) if the settlor has died and PETs have become taxable (3) if 18 March 1986 has intervened and seven years taxable transfers have to be substituted.

4.7:4   General rules for discretionary trusts

(a) No asset is to be counted twice. It would otherwise be possible for an asset to suffer an exit charge and later become relevant property again, thus appearing in both the 'snowball' and the 'transfer'.

(b) If, immediately the trust is set up, the settlor or his spouse or widow(er) has an interest in possession, the assets will not be treated as trust property until that interest comes to an end. This will not affect the dates of periodic charges but will affect the calculation of the effective rate.

4.8   EXEMPTIONS AND RELIEFS

4.8:1   An individual's lifetime exemptions

Annual exemption and the exemptions for marriage gifts are available after 5 April 1981 if a person having an interest in possession elects (within six months) to make them available (IHTA 1984, s 57) on an occasion when his interest ceases during his lifetime. If the assignment of an interest in possession satisfies the conditions as regards maintenance of a spouse, a child or a dependant relative (Appendix III Note IHT 10) the interest in possession will not be treated as coming to an end (IHTA 1984, s 51 (2)).

Other lifetime exemptions – small gifts and normal expenditure out of income are not available on the cessation of an interest in possession.

None of these exemptions is available to a discretionary trust.

4.8:2 An individual's exemptions during lifetime, or on death

The cessation of an interest in possession will be exempt where the trust assets or an interest in possession in those assets pass to:
(a) The spouse of the beneficiary whose interest ceases provided that spouse is domiciled in the UK.
(b) A charity, a political party or certain other bodies.
Where there is a transfer of a reversionary interest which has been purchased, these exemptions do not apply (IHTA 1984, s 56).
A trust without interest in possession cannot claim spouse exemption but where assets cease to be relevant property on transfer to a charity, a political party or certain other bodies there is no exit charge.

4.8:3 Surviving spouse exemption

Where one spouse died before 13 November 1974 and the surviving spouse has an interest in possession in assets which bore estate duty on the first death (or would have done if the value had been sufficient) then there is no IHT on the death of the surviving spouse (IHTA 1984, Sch 6, para 2).

4.8:4 Business relief

(a) *Business assets used by the trustees*
The business assets may be used by the trustees where they are carrying on a business. Provided the business, the assets and the period of ownership all qualify the trust will be entitled to 50% relief on an occasion of charge. This occasion may be the end of an interest in possession or a periodic charge or an exit charge.
(b) *Business assets used by the beneficiary*
On the other hand the business assets may be used by a beneficiary with an interest in possession where he (and not the trustee) is carrying on the business. Provided the business, the assets and the period of ownership all qualify, the trust will be entitled to 50% relief (and not 30%) on an occasion of charge; eg the death of the life tenant. *Fetherston haugh v IRC* [1984] STC 261.
(c) *Business assets used by a company*
Where the trust owns business assets which are used by a company controlled by the trustees or controlled by a beneficiary having an interest in possession, 30% relief is available if all the conditions are met.

(d) *Business assets used by a partnership*
Where the trust owns business assets used by a partnership in which one of the partners is a beneficiary having an interest in possession 30% relief is available if all the conditions are met.

(e) *Shares giving control*
Where the trustees control the company by virtue of their holding they will be entitled to 50% relief provided the business, the company and the period of ownership all qualify. Again the occasion of charge may be the end of an interest in possession, a periodic charge or an exit charge.

(f) *Unquoted shares not giving control*
If all conditions are met as above the trustees will be entitled to 30% relief (20% for transfers before 15 March 1983) on any occasion of charge.

For the application of the relief to partly exempt transfers – see Appendix III Note IHT 16.

Where the settlor's gift into trust attracted business relief and the settlor dies within seven years and after 17 March 1986 the calculation of tax on his death shall not take account of business relief unless the business assets or shares (or assets, or shares which replaced them) were owned by the trust from the date of gift to the date of death and were relevant business property at the latter date.

In the case of an interest in possession the period will end with the death of the tenant if earlier.

This provision can apply to part of the business property gifted into trust and not to another part (IHTA 1984, s 113A).

4.8:5   Agricultural relief

(a) *Property occupied by the beneficiary*
Where a beneficiary with an interest in possession occupies the property for the purposes of agriculture, he is treated as the owner in applying the rules for relief. Thus if he has occupied the property for two years there will be 50% relief on the ending of his interest in possession.

(b) *Property occupied by the trustees*
If the trustees have occupied the property for the purposes of agriculture for two years, 50% relief is available whether there is an interest in possession or not.

(c) *Property let*
Provided the property is occupied by someone for the purposes of agriculture, 30% relief will be available:

(1) if there is no interest in possession and the trust has owned the property for seven years; or

(2) a beneficiary has had an interest in possession for seven years.

Note 1 – For the application of the relief to partly exempt transfers – see Appendix III Note IHT 16.

Note 2 – The transitional relief operating since 10 March 1981 does not apply to discretionary trusts, but if a beneficiary with an interest in possession could have claimed the old 'working farmers' relief immediately before 10 March 1981 and if his interest and his occupation continue then the transitional relief is still available.

Note 3 – Where the settlor's gift into trust attracted agricultural relief and the settlor dies within seven years and after 17 March 1986, the calculation of tax on his death shall not take account of agricultural relief unless:

1   the property (or property which replaced it) was owned by the trust from the date of gift to the date of death; and

2   the property has been occupied for the purposes of agriculture for the same period.

In the case of an interest in possession the period will end with the death of the tenant if earlier.

This provision can apply to part of the property gifted into trust and not to another part. (IHTA 1984, s 124A).

4.8:6   Quick succession relief

Where an interest in possession comes to an end within five years after a chargeable occasion for the same property, there is relief against the later tax based on a percentage of the earlier tax. For events after 9 March 1981 the percentages are:

Not more than one year	100%
,, ,, ,, two years	80%
,, ,, ,, three ,,	60%
,, ,, ,, four ,,	40%
,, ,, ,, five ,,	20%

4.8:7   Woodlands relief

On the death of a beneficiary having an interest in possession there may be an election (where the asset is not agricultural property) to exclude growing timber (but not the land) from the calculation of tax.

When the timber is disposed of, the proceeds (or market value) are added to the total transfers on the earlier death and the additional tax thus created is payable by the person entitled – normally the trust. Where there is no election for relief there is no charge on the later disposal.

The relief is not available to discretionary trusts.

4.8:8   Payment of inheritance tax by instalments

An election to pay by ten annual instalments is available where there is an interest in possession in qualifying property (Appendix III Note IHT 11) and the occasion of charge is:
(a) the death of the 'tenant';
(b) the end of the interest in possession with the property remaining in the trust;
(c) a beneficiary who pays the tax becoming absolutely entitled to the property;
(d) the disposal of timber where woodlands relief has been claimed on an earlier death.

In the case of a discretionary trust the relief is available:
(a) where the property remains in trust – eg on a periodic charge or the creation of an interest in possession;
(b) where the property is distributed to a beneficiary who pays the tax.

Where a gift of qualifying property is a PET (eg a gift into an accumulation and maintenance trust) and the settlor dies within seven years, instalments are only available if the asset still belongs to the trust at the date of death.

4.9   POINTS RELEVANT TO PLANNING

Thus we can deduce the points which are most relevant to IHT planning:

4.9:1   A reversionary interest can be gifted without any tax liability.

4.9:2   A gift into a trust in which the settlor or his spouse has the interest in possession does not give rise to any tax liability.

4.9:3   It may be sensible to give the trustee of a fixed interest trust power to distribute capital to the life tenant.

4.9:4   Excluded property is a very suitable asset to be held by a fixed interest trust.

4.9:5   The sale of a life interest will produce less than the full value of the assets and will therefore give rise to a capital transfer.

4.9:6   The assets in a discretionary trust are not aggregated with the assets of the settlor or the beneficiaries.

4.9:7   A discretionary trust never pays IHT at death rates.

4.9:8   A discretionary trust formed without liability (eg because the settlor has not exceeded his zero-rate band) can probably make distributions without liability for the first ten years of its life.

4.9:9   In the same circumstances there will be no liability on the tenth anniversary if both the assets and the. zero-rate band have merely kept pace with inflation.

4.9:10   Additional property should be gifted into a new trust rather than added to an existing trust.

4.9:11   A absolute gift should be made after, rather than before, a gift into a discretionary trust.

4.9:12   A number of small discretionary trusts (made on different days) may generate less IHT then one large trust (Example **4.10:20**).

4.10   INHERITANCE TAX EXAMPLES

4.10:1   Example IHT 1 (see 4.2:1)

	£
Assets gifted into trust (measured as the loss to the settlor) where the trust suffers the tax	72,000
Annual exemption (if not already used)	3,000
	69,000
Taxable transfers by the settlor in the previous 7 years	95,000
	164,000

Tax at half rates on	164,000	=	16,550
Tax at half rates on	95,000	=	3,600
Tax at half rates on	£69,000	=	12,950

4.10:2   Example IHT 2 (see 4.2:1)

	£
Assets gifted into trust (measured as the loss to the settlor) where the settlor suffers the tax	72,000
Annual exemption (if not already used)	3,000
	69,000
Taxable transfers by the settlor in the previous 7 years	95,000
	164,000

Tax at 'grossed' half rates on	164,000	=	21,355	
Tax at 'grossed' half rates on	95,000	=	4,364	
Tax at 'grossed' half rates on	£69,000	=	16,991	16,991

In this example the settlor's estate suffers the gift of £69,000 and also the tax of £16,991 so that the problem is to find the tax on the total of the two ie £85,991. The calculation derives from the Tables as follows:

	£			£
Tax at 'grossed' half rates on	147,450		=	16,550
Tax at 'grossed' half rates on	16,550	@ 9/31	=	4,805
Tax at 'grossed' half rates on	164,000		=	21,355
Tax at 'grossed' half rates on	91,400		=	3,600
Tax at 'grossed' half rates on	3,600	@ 7/33	=	764
	95,000			4,364
	69,000			16,991

4.10:3 Example IHT 3 (see 4.2:4)

	£	£
Value of testator's estate at date of death		350,000
Less: Assets bequeathed to widow	100,000	
Assets bequeathed to charity	50,000	
		150,000
		200,000
Transfers by testator in previous 7 years (this could be a PET, a gift into trust, an interest in possession ceasing or indeed all three)		95,000
		295,000
Tax on £295,000 at full rates	98,400	
Tax on £95,000 at full rates	7,200	
Tax on £200,000	91,200	
Executors expenses	4,800	
		96,000
		199,000

Note that the tax on £95,000 is calculated at full rates although it might earlier have been paid at half rates.

Assets bequeathed to son	49,000
Residue left in trust for grandchildren	150,000

Note 1 The tax on the lifetime gift would be subject to tapering if the gift was made more than three years before death.

Note 2 If the lifetime gift bore tax at the time of gift, this is available as a credit.

Note 3 If any tax remains on the lifetime gift it is payable in the first instance by the donee, but with recourse to the estate.

4.10:4 Example IHT 4 (see 4.3:3 and 4.3:4)

End of 'interest in possession' (Appendix III Note IHT 2) on death of tenant.

	£
Market value of trust assets in which deceased had the interest	60,000
Market value of deceased's personal estate	70,000
	130,000

£

All transfers by deceased in previous 7 years
(see comments in **4.10:3**)   95,000

                                                                                225,000

	£		£	
Tax at full rates on	225,000	=	61,500	
Tax at full rates on	95,000	=	7,200	
Tax payable on	£130,000	=	54,300	(effective
rate 41.77%)				

Tax payable by trust on £60,000 at 41.77%   25,062

4.10:5   Example IHT 5 (see 4.3:5)

End of 'interest in possession' (Appendix III Note IHT 2) during
life of tenant.

£

Market value of trust assets in which tenant had the interest   83,000
Taxable transfers by tenant in previous 7 years   81,000

                                                                 164,000

	£		£
Tax at half rates on	164,000	=	16,550
Tax at half rates on	81,000	=	1,500
Tax payable by trust on	83,000	=	15,050

4.10:6   Example IHT 6 (see 4.5:2)

Periodic charge on trust assets in which there is no 'interest in
possession' (relevant property) where the settlement was made before
27 March 1974.

£

Market value of trust assets in which no one has an
'interest in possession' (relevant property – Appendix
III Note IHT 5)   115,000
'Transfers' (Appendix III Note IHT 6) by the trust in
previous 10 years (and after 26 March 1974)   91,000

                                                                 206,000

	£		£	
Tax at half rates on	206,000	=	26,000	
Tax at half rates on	91,000	=	3,000	
Tax at half rates on	115,000	=	23,000	(effective
rate 20%)				

Periodic charge at 30% of above (efffective rate 6%)   6,900

4.10:7   Example IHT 7 (see 4.5:3)

Transfer of relevant property (Appendix III Note IHT 5) between periodic charges where the settlement was made before 27 March 1974

	£
Market value of asset 'transferred' (Appendix III Note IHT 6)	40,000
Number of complete quarters since periodic charge – 10	
Effective rate of CTT on last periodic charge – 6% (Example **4.10:6**)	
Accrued portion thereof (10/40)	– 1.5%
Tax payable on transfer ('exit charge')	600

This example assumes that the same scale of rates applies at the transfer date. If there is a new scale in force it should be used.

4.10:8   Example IHT 8 (see 4.5:4)

Transfer of relevant property (Appendix III Note IHT 5) before the first periodic charge where the settlement was made before 27 March 1974.

	£
Market value of asset leaving trust (or otherwise) (Appendix III Note IHT 6)	30,000
Transfers (Note 6) by trust in last 10 years (and since 26/3/74)	95,000
	125,000

	£		£
Tax at lifetime rates on	125,000	=	8,850
Tax at lifetime rates on	95,000	=	3,600
Tax at lifetime rates on	30,000	=	5,250

CTT payable on transfer (exit charge) at 30% of above   1,575

Note If the 'transfer' was between 1 April 1980 and 31 March 1983 the charge was 20% of full CTT instead of 30%. Before 1 April 1980 there was a scale of transitional rates.

4.10:9   Example IHT 9 (see 4.5:5)

Periodic charge where property has become relevant property in a pre-27 March 1974 trust since the previous periodic charge.

	£
Market value of relevant property (including £10,000 which became relevant 15 quarters after the last periodic charge)	115,000
Periodic charge at 6.00% as in Example **4.10:6**	6,900
Less allowance on £10,000 at 6.00% x 15/40	225
	6,675

4.10:10   Example IHT 10 (see 4.5:6)

'Transfer' of relevant property between periodic charges where there has been an 'addition' since the previous periodic charge.

	£
Relevant property in the trust at the last periodic charge (valued at that date)	115,000
Property which became relevant since then (valued when added)	30,000
	145,000
Transfers by the trust in the 10 years preceding the last periodic charge	35,000
	180,000

	£		£
Tax at half rates on	180,000	=	20,150
Tax at half rates on	35,000	=	—
	145,000		20,150
Effective rate	13.9%		
30% thereof	4.17%		

Transfer of relevant property (Appendix III Note IHT 5) after the above addition of £30,000 and 22 quarters after the previous periodic charge £25,000

Exit charge at 4.17% x $\frac{22}{40}$ 573

4.10:11 Example IHT 11 (see **4.5:7**)

Periodic charge where the value of the trust has been increased (since the previous periodic charge) by a transfer by the settlor.

	£	£
Market value of relevant property (Appendix III Note IHT 5)		115,000
'Transfers' by the trust in the previous 10 years	£90,000	
Taxable transfers by the settlor in the 7 years preceding the transfer which increased the value of the trust	£20,000	110,000
		225,000

	£	£
Tax at half rates on	225,000 =	30,750
Tax at half rates on	110,000 =	6,225
Tax at half rates on	115,000	24,525

Effective rate	21.33%	
30% thereof	6.40%	
Periodic charge on £115,000 @ 6.40%		7,360
Less allowance on the addition for the number of quarters completed before it was added — £25,000 @ 6.40 x 15/40		600
		6,760

4.10:12 Example IHT 12 (see **4.5:8**)

Periodic charge where property is in the 'snowball' (the transfers of the previous 10 years) and has again become relevant property.

	£	£
Market value of relevant property (including £10,000 in respect of property in the 'snowball')		110,000
'Transfers' by the trust in the previous 10 years (including £8,000 in respect of the property which again became relevant)	98,000	
Less allowance for duplicated property (lower of £10,000 and £8,000)	8,000	
		90,000
		200,000

	£		£
Tax at half rates on	200,000	=	24,650
Tax at half rates on	90,000	=	2,850
Tax at half rates on	110,000		21,800

Effective rate	19.82%
30% thereof	5.95%

	£
Periodic charge on £110,000 @ 5.95%	6,545
Less allowance on the property again becoming relevant for the number of quarters completed before it did so £10,000 at 5.95% x 35/40	521
	6,024

4.10:13   Example IHT 13 (see 4.6:1, 4.6:2 and 4.6:3)

Periodic charge on trust assets in which there is no 'interest in possession' (relevant property) where the settlement was made after 26 March 1974.

	£
Market value of relevant property	110,000
Trust property which was never relevant (valued at the time it was settled)	30,000
Value of related trusts at the settlement date	—
	140,000

	£	
Transfers by the trust in the previous 10 years (and after 26 March 1974)	45,000	
Taxable transfers by the settlor in the 7 years preceding the settlement date	35,000	
		80,000
		220,000

	£		£
Tax at half rates on	220,000	=	29,500
Tax at half rates on	80,000	=	1,350
Tax at half rates on	140,000		28,150

Effective rate	20.11%	
Periodic charge on £110,000 at (30% x 20.11%) 6.03%		6,633

4.10:14 Example IHT 14 (see **4.6:6**)

Transfer of relevant property (Appendix III Note IHT 5) between periodic charges

	£
Market value of asset leaving trust (or otherwise) (Appendix III Note IHT 6)	40,000
Number of complete quarters since periodic charge – 14	
Effective rate of tax on last periodic charge – 6.03% (eg 13)	
Accrued proportion thereof 14/40 – 2.11%	
Tax payable on transfer (exit charge)	844

This example assumes that the same scale of rates applies at the transfer date. If there is a new scale it should be substituted.

4.10:15 Example IHT 15 (see **4.6:7**)

Transfer of relevant property (Appendix III Note IHT 5) before the first periodic charge where the settlement was made after 26 March 1974
Market value of asset leaving trust (or otherwise) (Appendix III Note IHT 6) £40,000

	£
Value of the whole trust at the time it was settled	110,000
Assets added between these dates valued when settled	30,000
Value of related trusts (Appendix III Note IHT 8) at the time they were settled	—
	140,000
Taxable transfers by settlor in 7 years pre-settlement	35,000
	175,000

	£		£
Tax at half rates on	175,000	=	19,025
Tax at half rates on	35,000	=	—
Tax at half rates on	140,000		19,025

Effective rate   13.59%
Full exit charge at 30% of effective rate 4.08%
Number of complete quarters since settlement date (or since the transferred property was added) – 12
12/40 x 4.08% = 1.22% (accrued proportion of exit charge)

Tax payable on transfer of £40,000 @ 1.22%	488

4.10:16   Example IHT 16 (see 4.6:7)

A discretionary trust formed without a CTT liability can exceptionally have a liability on 'transfers' before the first periodic charge

		£
Trust formed 15 June 1985 with shares value		146,000
Business relief at 50%		73,000
		73,000

	£	
Annual exemption for 1985/86	3,000	
Annual exemption for 1984/85	3,000	
Zero-rate band for 1985/86	67,000	
		73,000

'Transfer' on 15 January 1987 £73,000

	£
Value of trust when settled	146,000
Business relief at 30%	43,800
	102,200
Zero-rate band for 1986/87	71,000
	31,200
Tax @ 15% and 17.5%	4,860

Effective rate	4.76%
30% thereof	1.43%
6 quarters	
40 quarters	0.21%

This exit charge is applied to the market value of the property ceasing to be relevant less business relief ie £73,000 less £21,900 = £51,100 @ 0.21% – £107.

Another factor which can give rise to an exit charge in the first 10 years (where there was no tax on the gift into trust) is the existence of a related settlement.

4.10:17   Example IHT 17 (see 4.6:8)

Periodic charge where additional property has become relevant in a post 26 March 1974 trust since the previous periodic charge.

	£
Market value of relevant property (including £10,000 which became relevant 16 quarters after the previous periodic charge)	110,000
Periodic charge at 6.03% as in Example **4.10:13**	6,633
Less allowance on £10,000 at 16/40 x 6.03%	241
	6,392

4.10:18   Example IHT 18 (see 4.6:9)

'Transfer' of relevant property between periodic charges where there has been an 'addition' since the previous periodic charge.

	£
Relevant Property in the trust at the last periodic charge (valued at that time)	120,000
Property which has become relevant since then (valued when added)	20,000
Trust property which was never relevant (valued when settled)	35,000
Assets in related trusts (valued when settled)	—
	175,000

	£	
'Transfers' by the trust in the 10 years preceding the last periodic charge	45,000	
Taxable transfers by the settlor in the 7 years preceding the settlement date	35,000	
	80,000	
	255,000	

	£		£
Tax at half rates on	255,000	=	38,250
Tax at half rates on	80,000	=	1,350
	175,000	=	36,900
Effective rate	21.09%		
30% thereof	6.33%		

'Transfer' of relevant property after the above addition of £20,000 and 22 quarters after the previous periodic charge £25,000

Exit charge at 6.33% x 22/40	870

4.10:19   Example IHT 19 (see **4.6:10**)

Periodic charge where the value of the trust has been increased (since the previous periodic charge) by a transfer by the settlor.

	£
Market value of the relevant property	110,000
Trust property which was never relevant (valued when settled)	30,000
Assets in related trusts (valued when settled)	—
	140,000

	£	
'Transfers' by the trust in the previous 10 years	55,000	
Taxable transfers by the settlor in the 7 years preceding the settlement date £25,000		
Taxable transfers by the settlor in the 7 years preceding the transfer which increased the value of the trust (substituted because greater)	45,000	
	100,000	
	240,000	

	£		£
Tax at half rates on	240,000	=	34,500
Tax at half rates on	100,000	=	4,475
Tax at half rates on	140,000	=	30,025

Effective Rates	21.45%	
30% thereof	6.43%	
Periodic charge on £110,000 @ 6.43%		7,073
Less allowance on the addition for the number of quarters completed before it was added – £25,000 @ 6.43% x 15/40		603
		6,470

4.10:20   Example IHT 20 (see **4.6:10**, **4.9:12** and **7.4:9(a)**)

Comparing the liability of three small trusts (made on different days) with the liability of one large trust.

(a) One trust with assets value £75,000 at settlement date.

	£
Value on tenth anniversary	150,000
Trust's transfers in previous 10 years	—
Settlor's transfers in 7 years pre-trust	—
	—
	150,000
Tax thereon	13,750

Effective rate	9.17%
30% thereof	2.75%
Periodic charge £150,000 x 2.75% =	4,125

(b) Three smaller trusts each with assets value £25,000 at settlement date.

	Trust A £	Trust B £	Trust C £
Value on tenth anniversary	50,000	50,000	50,000
Trusts' transfers	—	—	—
Settlor's transfers pre-trust	—	25,000	50,000
	—	25,000	50,000
	50,000	75,000	100,000

Note The first trust will form the settlor's snowball for the second and the total of the two for the third.

	Trust A	Trust B	Trust C
Tax thereon	—	600	4,475
Tax on 'snowball'	—	—	—
	—	600	4,475
Effective rate	—	1.20%	8.95%
30% thereof	—	0.36%	2.68%
Periodic charge	—	£180	£1,340

Total periodic charge	£1,520

This represents a saving of £2,605 but has to be considered against the extra costs of administration etc.

4.10:21   Example IHT 21 (see **4.6:11**)

Periodic charge where property is in the 'snowball' (the 'transfers' of the previous 10 years) and has again become relevant property.

		£
Market value of relevant property (including £10,000 in respect of property in the 'snowball')		110,000
Trust property which was never relevant (valued when settled)		30,000
Assets in related trusts (valued when settled)		—
		140,000

	£	
'Transfers' by the trust in the previous 10 years (including £8,000 in respect of property which again became relevant	45,000	
Less allowance for duplicated property (lower of £10,000 and £8,000)	8,000	
	37,000	
Taxable transfers by the settlor in the 7 years preceding the settlement date	40,000	
		77,000
		217,000

	£		£
Tax at half rates on	217,000	=	28,750
Tax at half rates on	77,000	=	900
Tax at half rates on	140,000		27,850

Effective rate	19.89%	
30% thereof	5.97%	
Periodic charge on £110,000 @ 5.97 =		6,567
Less allowance for property which became relevant 21 complete quarters after the previous periodic charge £10,000 x 5.97% x 21/40		313
		6,254

Chapter 5   Specialised Trusts

5.1   ACCUMULATION AND MAINTENANCE TRUSTS – IHTA 1984, s 71

5.1:1   Introduction

These trusts – known sometimes as 'super trusts' – are basically a method of benefiting minors by means of a discretionary trust without paying three lots of IHT – one into trust and one (or more) periodic charge and one exit charge.

They must start off as discretionary (no interest in possession) with the trustees having power to make payments out of income for the maintenance, education etc of the beneficiaries and power to accumulate the balance.

The beneficiaries must take interests in possession at an age not exceeding 25. Accumulation beyond the minority of a beneficiary may offend against the rules set out in **1.3:2** and it is safer to give interests in possession at age 18. The extent of the interests may also be at the trustees' discretion. They may take absolute interests at the stated age or later or at the trustees' discretion, or they may have life interests only. A power to revoke will disqualify a trust from IHTA 1984, s 71 – *Inglewood v IRC* [1981] STC 318.

The class of beneficiaries must be limited and the widest class is normally one where all are grandchildren of one grandparent or children or widow(er)s of beneficiaries who died before the specified age. There must be at least one beneficiary alive when the trust is formed – the others can be born later. An adopted child, a step child and an illegitimate child all count.

5.1:2   Income tax

The trust is initially discretionary and is therefore liable to investment income surcharge and to tax on excess distributions. A beneficiary's income is the payments to him grossed up by 45% tax. Payments to an unmarried infant child of the settlor are treated as the settlor's income.

When the eldest beneficiary reaches the specified age, the class should close and thereafter part of the income will be his for income tax purposes and no longer liable as discretionary. Example **2.8:11** shows a trust where one beneficiary has come of age and the other has not. In due course all beneficiaries will be entitled to income as of right and the discretionary trust provisions will cease to apply.

When a beneficiary reaches the stated age and becomes entitled to his share of accumulated income, he takes it as capital without any income tax consequences. While this can be advantageous, it is also worth considering paying out income each year if the beneficiaries are not liable to tax and can therefore recover the 45%.

5.1:3 Capital gains tax

The gift into trust is liable to CGT as explained and may be subject to an election for 'hold-over'.

When a beneficiary takes his interest in possession there is no CGT liability. When he takes an absolute interest there is a capital gain but it may be 'held-over' if the beneficiary is resident in the UK.

5.1:4 Inheritance tax

Until 17 March 1986 the gift into trust was liable to CTT in the normal way. From 18 March 1986 it is treated in the same way as a gift to an individual – that is to say there is no liability unless the settlor dies within seven years.

The trust itself has no liability, and in particular:

(a) when a beneficiary takes an interest in possession;
(b) when a beneficiary takes an absolute interest;
(c) when a beneficiary dies before taking an interest;
(d) on the tenth anniversary of the settlement (or the twentieth etc).

Thus this type of trust has great advantages from an IHT point of view.

Where however a beneficiary takes a further interest after the stated age there will be a liability. This could happen if a beneficiary who had not reached the stated age renounced or died or the trustees exercised discretion against him, and others over the stated age got his share or part of it.

There are also liabilities which apply in all cases:

(a) On the death of a beneficiary after reaching the stated age and acquiring his interest.
(b) On the trustees exercising a power to take away a beneficiary's interest after he has acquired it. It would seem that the existence of such a power does not disqualify the trust from enjoying the 'super trust' advantages.

5.2   PROTECTIVE TRUSTS – IHTA 1984, s 8

5.2:1   Introduction

These are really a way of protecting the trust against a beneficiary, or protecting him against himself. An improvident beneficiary might sell his interest or give it away. Or a trustee in bankruptcy might seek to take an interest.

A discretionary trust would prevent these happenings but would suffer investment income surcharge and periodic charges.

A protective trust gives the 'principal beneficiary' an interest in possession which ceases if he attempts to alienate his interest or if an outsider attempts to take an interest. The trust then becomes discretionary with a class of beneficiaries set out in the deed or (failing that) in the Trustee Act 1925. It has been held that the deed merely has to use the words 'on protective trust' to bring the provisions of the Act into the deed.

On the death of the 'principal' beneficiary the original provisions of the deed operate as regards the remainderman or succeeding life tenant.

5.2:2   Income tax

There are no special provisions relating to protective trusts. The exercise of protection will bring in the investment income surcharge and the tax on excess distributions and change the calculation of the beneficiary's statutory income. If the trust becomes discretionary this cannot include power to accumulate income.

5.2:3   Capital gains tax

There are no special CGT provisions relating to protective trusts.
The exercise of protection is not a disposal for CGT.

5.2:4   Inheritance tax

The exercise of protection is ignored for IHT provided that the capital ultimately goes back to the 'principal beneficiary'. That is to say his interest in possession is deemed to continue, and that will also exempt the trust from periodic charges. Any capital that goes to another beneficiary is treated as a capital transfer. If the principal beneficiary should die after the exercise of protection and before the capital distribution, the interest in possession which is deemed to continue will be treated as part of his estate.

5.3 MARRIAGE TRUSTS – IHTA 1984, s 22

5.3:1 Introduction

These are trusts set up prior to and in consideration of marriage. The beneficiaries can be the parties to the marriage, their children and the spouses of their children. It is also possible to include a subsequent spouse of either party and subsequent children and their spouses.

They can be discretionary, fixed interest or protective trusts.

5.3:2 Income tax

The rule which deems income to be that of the settlor (if income or capital can revert to him or his spouse) is waived in the case of a marriage trust if the reversion can only take place on the death of both parties to the marriage and all or any of their children.

5.3:3 Capital gains tax

There are no special provisions relating to marriage trusts.

5.3:4 Inheritance tax

Provided the class of beneficiaries stated above is not extended the gift into trust can attract an additional exemption. This is £5,000 in the case of a parent of one party, and £2,500 in the case of a grandparent. The exemption of £1,000 available to others does not apply to a gift into trust. Thus the parents of one party would have two exemptions of £5,000 each and two annual exemptions of £3,000 each – a total exemption of £16,000.

5.4   TRADING TRUSTS

5.4:1   Introduction

These are used in place of trading companies for the following reasons:

(a) Apportionment of income does not apply (this is not so important now that trading income is not apportionable).

(b) A beneficiary's interest is not liable to CGT (so that double taxation cannot arise as in the case of shares in a company).

(c) A beneficiary's interest cannot be caught under TA 1970, s 460 (transactions in securities).

(d) The trust is not subject to TA 1970, s 482 (company requires treasury consent to becoming non-resident).

5.4:2   Income tax

A beneficiary's income from the trust is not earned income (even though it is trading profit) and so there may be no point in interests in possession. However, if it is discretionary the same rule will operate to make the income liable to investment income surcharge.

5.4:3   Capital gains tax

The trust would be entitled to roll-over relief on the replacement of business assets.

No retirement relief would be available as it is the trust and not the beneficiary that is trading.

5.4:4   Inheritance tax

On any occasion of charge the trust would be entitled to business relief in respect of assets used for the purposes of the trade. This reduces the value of such assets by 50% provided the conditions are satisfied about the period of ownership, the period of use and the absence of a contract for sale (see **4.8:4**).

Where the trust's trade is one of farming, the property would similarly be entitled to agricultural relief of 50% in most circumstances (see **4.8:5**).

5.5 INSURANCE TRUSTS

These trusts are so called because the assets in the trustee's hands consist of insurance policies of one kind or another. We will consider each type separately as each has a different purpose and a different tax position.

5.5:1 Inheritance trusts formed before 18 March 1986

In this first type the capital in the trustee's hands was invested in single premium life policies. These are referred to in the insurance world as 'investment bonds' or 'growth bonds' and in the tax legislation as 'non-qualifying life policies'.

The normal procedure is to withdraw an annual amount not exceeding 5% of the original investment and pay it to the settlor as a loan or the repayment of a loan. This annual amount is not income of the trust or of the settlor.

However, if the annual withdrawals exceed 5% (on a cumulative basis) the excess is treated as the settlor's income (if he is alive) for the purposes of higher rates.

There are two basic types – firstly those where the capital was gifted to the trust and the annual withdrawals are paid to the settlor as loans. In the second type the trust was formed with a small gift and the main capital was loaned to the trust (free of interest and repayable on demand) and the annual withdrawals are used as part repayments. The insurance companies withdrew these schemes following the 1986 Budget, but existing trusts are protected by the transitional provisions. As there are a very large number in existence they are considered in some detail.

Income tax

The annual withdrawals are not income and the annual loans or repayments have no income tax effect so long as the trust has no undistributed income. For this reason (among others) such trusts normally have no other type of investment. There must of course be some risk of the Revenue seeking to treat the annual payments to the settlor as income and claiming tax under FA 1973, s 17. For this reason (among others) the beneficiary should have an interest in possession – s 17 only applies to discretionary trusts.

When the bond matures or is surrendered or sold the total gain is calculated (including the annual withdrawals) and the settlor is assessed to the excess of his top rate over the basic rate on a 'top-slicing' basis. For example, if the bond cost £10,000 and 5% (£500) was withdrawn each year for ten years and the bond then realised £14,000, the total proceeds would be £500 x 10 plus £14,000 or a total of £19,000. Deducting the cost of £10,000 the gain becomes £9,000. If the bond lasted ten complete years the annual equivalent is £900. Adding £900 to the settlor's income (in the year in which the gain was realised) increases his tax by (say) £500. Deducting basic rate tax of £261 there is an excess liability of £239. The total liability for ten years is therefore £2,390. The basic rate tax is notional and cannot be reclaimed or used to cover annual payments. If the settlor is entitled to age relief, this may be affected.

It may be possible to avoid these problems by assigning the bond to a beneficiary before the gain arises, if he would not have a higher rate liability. It is the ownership of the bond at the date the gain arises which is the deciding factor.

If the settlor is dead when the gain is realised it would seem that no liability can arise, and for this reason the bond may be written on a 'joint life last survivor' basis with a beneficiary as the other life. Such beneficiary would have to be over 12 years old.

If the bond terminates on death the 'death benefit' (excess over the cash value) is free of all tax. That is to say the gain is based on the surrender value immediately prior to death.

Capital gains tax

The gain on the bond is not liable to CGT unless the bond was bought second-hand before 26 June 1982.

Inheritance tax

In the first type the gift into trust was liable to IHT in the ordinary way. The annual loans to the settlor build up a liability and (if spent as income) reduce his estate further without any tax liability. The trust may be liable to periodic charge unless there is an interest in possession. This interest may have no other consequences as the bond produces no income for the tenant to claim. The existence of this interest in possession will also prevent an 'exit charge' when the beneficiary gets an absolute interest.

In the second type the loan into trust had no IHT consequences. The loan is an asset of the settlor's estate and the annual repayments reduce that asset and (if they are spent as income) reduce his total estate. As the trust acquires value by reduction of the loan (and hopefully by increase in the value of the bond) it may become liable to the periodic charge and so it may be desirable for the beneficiary to have an interest in possession. As in the first type the existence of an interest in possession has little effect other than the avoidance of the periodic charge and the exit charge when a beneficiary gets an absolute interest.

It is normal for the settlor to be a potential beneficiary and for the trustee to have the power to appoint capital to him and thus away from the 'tenant'.

The introduction of the rules about 'gifts with reservation' and 'non-deductible debts' on 18 March 1986 resulted in these schemes being withdrawn, but existing trusts are protected under the transitional provisions which provide that the new rules do not apply to gifts made and debts created before 18 March 1986 (see **4.1:8**). Thus the interest reserved will not result in the policy being part of the settlor's estate if he survives his gift by seven years. Even if he does not survive it will be the amount of his gift that will be counted and not the current value of the policy.

The transitional provisions also protect gifts made after 17 March 1986 under the terms of regular premium policies effected before 18 March 1986, and not varied since (FA 1986, s 102(6)).

5.5:2   Inheritance trusts formed after 17 March 1986

At the time of writing the insurance companies have not commenced marketing of any new version of these schemes due mainly to uncertainty as to the party liable to any IHT arising on death within seven years. But there seems no reason why new trusts should not hold 'growth bonds' provided the settlor does not make himself one of the beneficiaries, or expect loans from the trust to be deductible from his estate on death.

The advantages of withdrawals up to 5% without immediate tax liability still remain. Where withdrawals are not required there is an advantage of accumulation without investment income surcharge or periodic charge or exit charge.

Income tax

The liability on the maturity or surrender of the bond is as described under **5.5:1**. The comments about assignment of the bond and the death of the settlor still apply.

Capital gains tax

The gain is not liable to CGT.

Inheritance tax

The rules about gifts with reservation which were introduced on 18 March 1986 mean that if the settlor is a potential beneficiary, the policy (bond) will remain part of his estate and if he dies without having surrendered his potential interest the policy will be liable at death rates on its value at the date of death.

Thus such 'reservation' is not sensible and a settlor will no longer have the chance of getting his capital back.

The gift into trust is liable to IHT in the normal way and an interest in possession can still prevent periodic and exit charges.

All IHT liability (including that on the gift into trust) can be avoided if the trust observes the rules as an accumulation and maintenance settlement (see **5.1**) and this seems the route that the insurance companies are likely to take.

5.5:3 PETA plans

These schemes (also known as discounted gift schemes) were also withdrawn by the insurance companies following the 1986 Budget. There are two life insurance policies involved – a pure endowment and a term assurance – hence the name PETA. Most of the capital (perhaps 99%) went into the single premium endowment policy which matures on the taxpayer living to 105; thus it is very unlikely to mature at all. However, the settlor retains the right to make partial surrenders of the policy to provide his 5% 'income' each year.

The other policy (which is linked) is a term assurance with a single premium accounting for the small balance of the amount invested. In the unlikely event of the endowment maturing, the term assurance pays nothing, but on the settlor's death before the endowment date the term policy pays the then value of the units purchased by the endowment premium.

It was the term policy which was settled in trust for the beneficiary who should have an interest in possession. If the settlor was worried that his circumstances might change, the trustees could be given the power to appoint the interest away from the beneficiary.

Income tax

The term assurance (ie the policy in trust) is a non-qualifying policy but on death there is no higher rate liability as there is in the inheritance trusts, because it is based on the surrender value immediately prior to death and the PETA term assurance has no surrender value (IHTA 1970, s 395 (1)(a)).

Capital gains tax

No liability can arise in normal circumstances.

Inheritance tax

The settlor's estate was reduced when he entered into the arrangement and the future growth in the value of the units is outside his estate.

Plans entered into before 18 March 1986 are protected by the transitional provisions so that the interest reserved will not result in the policy being part of the settlor's estate if he survives seven years.

Some well-known insurance companies did not offer PETA plans because of their artificial nature and the likelihood of a Revenue attack. Whether the Revenue will still attack them under the pre-1986 law remains to be seen.

5.5:4   Inheritance tax funding

In this type there is no gift or loan of a lump sum into trust. The trustees hold an ordinary whole of life policy on the life of the settlor the purpose of which is to provide the cash to meet the IHT arising on the settlor's death. The policy is in trust for the beneficiary.

As the policy is not the property of the deceased, the proceeds can be paid out on proof of death without having to await the grant of probate.

Income tax

As the settlor is paying normal annual premiums on his own life the trust holds a qualifying policy and there is therefore no liability when the policy matures on his death. If the policy was taken out before 14 March 1984 tax relief of 15% can still be deducted from the payment of each annual premium. In some cases it is possible to write the policy under TA 1970, s 226A and so to make top-rate tax relief available.

Capital gains tax

No liability can arise on a qualifying life policy.

Inheritance tax

As the policy does not form part of the settlor's estate the annual premiums are gifts into trust. However in most cases they will be covered by the annual exemption of £3,000 or by the exemption of normal annual expenditure out of income.

The advantage of the policy being outside the settlor's estate is of course that there is no IHT liability on his death.

Where there has been a lifetime gift there should be additional temporary insurance to cover the additional tax which would arise on death within seven years of the gift.

Where assets have been left by one spouse to the other there is no tax on the first death and the trust policy will be a 'joint life last survivor' so that the cash is payable when the liability arises, ie on the second death.

Where there is more than one trust for more than one beneficiary they should be made on different days to avoid being related property.

5.5:5   Other types

There is no limit to the types of insurance policy which can be written in trust but other common examples are:

(a) A TA 1970, s 226A policy – that is a temporary life cover for a self-employed death-in-service benefit.
(b) The return of the fund backing a personal pension policy in the event of death-in-service.
(c) The return of the capital invested at the end of a guaranteed income bond.
(d) The 'back-to-back' life policy taken out to replace the capital invested in an annuity.

Note   In the case of an approved pension scheme or pension policy, death benefits payable under discretionary trusts are not liable to IHT, nor will the declaration of trust be a gift with reservation.

5.6   TRUSTS FOR EMPLOYEES – IHTA 1984, s 86

5.6:1   These trusts are formed for the benefit of all or most of the employees of a body carrying on a trade or profession and/or for their spouses, relatives or dependants. The terms must provide that none of the settled property can be applied for the benefit of a participator in the employer company or in another company which has made a transfer into the trust or who has been such a participator within the ten years before the transfer, or who is a person connected with such a participator.

For this purpose a participator will not include one who owns or has rights over less than 5% of any class of the issued shares. A participator in an open company is included.

Any settled property applied for the benefit of a participator is ignored if treated as his income (or would be if he were resident).

For events after 8 March 1982 the trust will qualify if it is approved under FA 1978, Sch 9 as a profit sharing scheme.

5.6:2 Income tax

There are no special provisions. If such a trust is wound up and cash distributed, this will be taxable even if the recipients' employment has ceased. This could arise on a take-over for cash (*Bray v Best* (1986) FTR 28/1/86).

5.6:3 Capital gains tax

(a) A gift into the trust by an individual is exempt from CGT if:
   (1) it is made after 10 April 1978;
   (2) it consists of shares in the company;
   (3) within one year of the transfer the trust holds more than half the ordinary shares in the company and the trustees have a majority of the votes.
(b) A gift of any asset into the trust by a close company does not give rise to a chargeable gain if made after 6 April 1976.
(c) A gift of any asset by an open company is also exempt.

5.6:4 Inheritance tax

(a) A transfer into the trust by an individual is exempt from IHT if it is exempt from CGT under **5.6:3(a).**
(b) A transfer of any asset into the trust by a close company after 6 April 1976 is not a transfer of value for IHT.
(c) A transfer into the trust by another discretionary trust does not give rise to a proportionate charge to IHT if made after 8 March 1982 and conditions (2) and (3) for individual settlors are satisfied.
The assets of the trust will not be relevant property and therefore there will be no periodic charges or exit charges.
There will still be a charge to tax on a transfer for the benefit of:
   (1) the settlor unless he settled not more than £1,000 per year;

(2) where the employer is a close company, a participator subject to the 5% rule as above;

(3) a person who has acquired an interest for money or money's worth;

(4) a person connected with any of the above.

There can also be a charge on property which does not leave the trust but ceases to be held subject to the qualifying conditions.

Where a charge arises the tax is calculated on a tapered scale dependent on how many quarters the assets have been held on the exempt trusts after 13 March 1975:

0.25% for each of the first 40 complete quarters

0.2% for each of the next 40 complete quarters

0.15% for each of the next 40 complete quarters

0.1% for each of the next 40 complete quarters

0.05% for each of the next 40 complete quarters

Thus the charge starts at 1% per annum and tapers to 0.2% per annum.

There are provisions for continuity (without tax liability) where the trust is terminated and the assets transferred into another qualifying trust.

While these trusts are basically discretionary, an interest in possession not exceeding 5% of the assets is ignored.

5.7   NEWSPAPER TRUSTS (IHTA 1984, s 87)

5.7:1   These are trusts whose principal property (Appendix III Note IHT 13) is shares in a newspaper publishing company, that is to say a company whose business consists mainly in the publication of a newspaper in the UK. Shares in a holding company will qualify if the principal asset of that company is shares in a newspaper publishing company and if the holding company has the majority of votes on most questions affecting the subsidiary as a whole.

Some well-known newspapers such as the Guardian and the Manchester Evening News come under these provisions.

5.7:2   Income tax

There are no special provisions.

5.7:3   Capital gains tax

There are no special provisions.

5.7:4   Inheritance tax

Where the trust is formed for the benefit of a newspaper publishing company:

(a) A transfer into the trust by an individual will not be liable to tax if it is made after 10 April 1978 and it consists of shares in the company and within one year of the transfer the trust holds a majority of the ordinary shares and of the votes.

(b) Property in the trust will not be relevant property and there will only be a charge to tax in the case of a transfer for the benefit of any of the parties set out in **5.6:4**.

5.8   TRUSTS FOR THE DISABLED (IHTA 1984, s 89)

5.8:1   These are trusts where the property is held for the benefit of a mentally disabled person (ie one incapable of administering his property or managing his affairs) or a person in receipt of attendance allowance under the Social Security Acts. The terms of the trust must secure that where property is applied at least half is applied for the benefit of the disabled person.

5.8:2   Income tax

There are no special features.

5.8:3   Capital gains tax

The trust will be entitled to the same annual exemption as an individual (£6,300) instead of half that amount. There is, however, an additional condition that the terms of the trust must either entitle the disabled person to at least half the trust income or provide that no income can be applied for the benefit of another.

Where more than one such settlement is made by the same settlor after 9 March 1981, the annual exemption is divided between them subject to a minimum of £1,260.

5.8:4   Inheritance tax

Where the gift into trust is after 17 March 1986 it is treated as a gift to an individual.

Where the gift into trust is after 9 March 1981 and there is no interest in possession the disabled person is deemed to have such an interest and in consequence:

(a) If the disabled person is the settlor, the gift into trust is not a capital transfer.

(b) Capital distributions to him are not capital transfers.

On the other hand the following are capital transfers:

(a) Capital distributions to others.

(b) The death of the disabled person.

The relief is not withheld because of the existence of a statutory power of advancement under the Trustee Acts.

Where the disabled person has an interest in possession in the whole property the relief is not required.

Where another has an interest in possession in any of the property the relief is not available.

Different rules apply where the settlement took place before 10 March 1981.

Chapter 6   Overseas Trusts (Non-Resident Trusts)

6.1   INTRODUCTION

6.1:1   Certain tax provisions apply only to UK residents and it is possible for a trust as well as an individual to be (or to become) non-resident. A trust is non-resident if a majority of the trustees are neither resident nor ordinarily resident in the UK and the administration of the trust is carried on abroad.

6.1:2   Strictly speaking, however, the foregoing is the definition for CGT (CGTA 1979, s 52 (1)) (Appendix II Note CGT 10) and IHT (IHTA 1984, ss 201(5) and 218(3)) and it should be approached with caution for income tax purposes. There is no statutory definition of a non-resident trust for income tax purposes and it seems that because the trustees are a single body the UK residence of one can result in the UK residence of the body. Thus where there is a possibility of income tax saving, all the trustees (rather than a majority) should be non-resident to prevent a resident trustee being assessed in respect of overseas income.

6.1:3   Even with CGT it is better (when appointing funds to non-resident trustees) to leave no trustee of the orginal settlement resident in the UK (*Roome v Edwards* [1981] STC 96).

6.2   INCOME TAX

6.2:1   Introduction

The income tax treatment of non-resident trusts is based almost entirely on case law. There are a few statutory provisions and these, for example, deny to a non-resident trust:
(a) tax credits on UK dividends (FA 1972, s 86);
(b) repayment supplements (F (No 2) A 1975, s 47(11));
(c) relief from tax on non-resident life policies (FA 1984, Sch 15, para 8(3)). (Appendix I Note IT 13).

Income

6.2:2   Most of the trust income arising in the UK will have borne basic rate tax at source:
(a) Rental income will be subject to deduction of tax by the person who remits it out of the UK (TA 1970, s 89). The Schedule A expenses can first be deducted and perhaps interest (see **6.2:7b**).

(b) Interest on most gilts will be paid under deduction of tax and the Revenue will only agree to interest on exempt gilts being paid in full to a non-resident trust if a non-resident beneficiary has an interest in possession. For discretionary trusts see **6.2:6**.

(c) Bank and building society interest will suffer tax under the composite rate scheme unless a very restrictive declaration can be lodged (see Appendix I Note IT 18).

(d) Interest and dividends from UK companies will suffer tax in the normal way.

6.2:3 UK source income which is received in full can be assessed on any branch or agent whether they receive the income or not (TMA 1970, s 78). This will include the profits of a trade carried on through a branch or agency in the UK.

Where there is no agent in the UK the assessments will be raised on the trustees and where there are collection difficulties the Revenue can proceed not only against trust assets in the UK but also the personal UK assets of the trustees.

Note In practice the Revenue will not pursue the tax on UK interest where the beneficiary is non-resident (concession *B.13*). Nor will they pursue a resident agent who does not have management and control of the interest.

6.2:4 The Revenue rely on decisions of the courts (eg *Baker v Archer – Shee* (1927) 11TC 764) for their practice of taxing the income of a non-resident trust on a 'look-through' basis by reference to the residence status of a beneficiary who is absolutely entitled to the trust income.

Thus when the beneficiary is resident in the UK the revenue will assess overseas income on the trustees.

Where the beneficiary is resident but not domiciled in the UK (Appendix I Note IT 14) the overseas income will only be assessed if it is remitted to the UK – *Williams v Singer* (1921) 7 TC 409.

6.2:5 Where the beneficiary is not entitled to the whole trust income but only to a fractional share of it the legal position is less clear. It seems however that the different shares can be treated in different ways.

Thus, in *Reids Trustees v IRC* (1929) 14 TC 512 Lord Clyde concluded:

'trustees may have a good answer to a particular assessment as regards some share or part of the income on the ground that such share or part accrues beneficially to a (person) in whose hands it is not liable'.

6.2:6   In the case of a discretionary trust where no beneficiary has a right to receive income, the residence of the trust will determine the tax position. Thus where no trustee is resident in the UK:

(a)   overseas income will not be assessed;

(b)   interest paid in full on gilts will not be assessed;

(c)   interest on exempt gilts will be paid under deduction of tax, but if the trustees make returns showing that the income has been accumulated or paid to non-residents, the tax will be repaid to the trust;

(d)   building society interest will be paid in full if the trustees can supply the bank or the society with a declaration that all beneficiaries are individuals and are not ordinarily resident (SI 1986/182) (Appendix I Note IT 18);

(e)   bank interest is paid in full to all discretionary trusts – resident or non-resident.

6.2:7   Outgoings

The basic rule is that payments under all four headings (**2.3:1** to **2.3:4**) are dealt with as expenses and the total apportioned between the income which is liable to UK tax and that which is exempt in proportion to their gross amounts. The purpose of this apportionment is to arrive at the net UK income and this may be needed (1) if the beneficiary is non-resident (Example **2.8:12**) or (2) if there is a liability to investment income surcharge (Example **2.8:13**). The exceptions are:

(a)   Annual payments made in the UK may be subject to deduction of tax at source.

(b)   Interest on a loan for the purchase or improvement of property in the UK let at a commercial rent is allowable at Schedule A in the usual way.

Thus these exceptions are deducted from the gross income and not the net.

6.2:8   The beneficiary's income

Where a UK resident beneficiary is entitled to the income (ie he has an interest in possession) he is liable to UK tax on the whole net income (or his fractional share of it) subject to credit for the UK tax paid by the trust. If he is domiciled abroad (Appendix I Note IT 14) his UK tax will be on a remittances basis as regards foreign income. He may also be liable on 'benefits' (**6.2:11** (c)). Where the beneficiary is non-resident he is liable only on the UK part of the income less expenses (Example **2.8:12**).

6.2:9   Discretionary trusts

The investment income surcharge payable by the trustees (FA 1973, s 16) is charged on the liable income as above less the appropriate proportion of the expenses – see *IRC v Regent Trust Co Ltd* [1980] STC 140. The trust would not be entitled to the tax credit on UK dividends and the surcharge would therefore be on the actual net dividends only (FA 1972, s 85(5)) (Example **2.8:13**).

The resident beneficiary who receives income at the trustees' discretion is liable in respect of all that income irrespective of where it arises (*Drummond v Collins* (1915) 6TC 525). His liability is according to the year of payment. If he is domiciled abroad (Appendix I Note IT 14) his liability is on a remittances basis (TA 1970, s 122). In other words: the Revenue regard the trust itself as the source.

Beneficiary's 'look-through' relief can apply under Concession B18 if the trustees make fully vouched returns and pay the investment income surcharge.

Where the income falls to be assessed on the beneficiary the assessments are under Case V on a preceding year basis subject to commencement etc provisions. Again this is because the source is the trust itself.

Tax liability on excess income distributions does not arise unless the trustees place themselves within the provisions eg to get 'look-through' relief for a beneficiary.

6.2:10   Trusts ineffective for income tax

The deeming provisions set out in the main chapter on Income Tax apply to overseas trusts (**2.7**). Where the settlor is not domiciled (Appendix I Note IT 14) see **8.2:1.**

Where an overseas trust owns shares in a non-resident 'close' company, undistributed income of that company may be deemed income of the trust (TA 1970, s 451(1)). Thus a settlor both resident and domiciled in the UK may be chargeable on such income.

6.2:11   Additional anti-avoidance provisions

There are other provisions which affect overseas trusts and apply where there has been a 'transfer of assets' and as a result income has become payable to a non-resident. This clearly applies to the settlement of funds in an overseas trust and the resultant income of that trust, or of a non-resident company in which the trust owns shares.

The provisions do not apply where the transfer was a bona fide commercial transaction and not for tax avoidance and while it would be difficult for a settlement of funds in an overseas trust to claim this exemption, it would not be impossible. Protection of the assets or avoidance of exchange control might be valid defences.

There are four separate provisions charging individuals who are ordinarily resident in the UK:

(a) Where the person who transferred the assets (normally the settlor) or that person's spouse has in consequence 'power to enjoy' (Appendix I Note IT 15) the income of a non-resident (ie the overseas trust or an overseas company owned by the trustees) that income is assessible on that transferor (TA 1970, s 478). The provision cannot apply after the death of the transferor. Nor does it apply if the transferror would have no liability (eg as a non-resident).

The case of *Vestey v IRC* (1980) STC 10 decided that s 478 does not apply to a non-transferor.

(b) Where the person who transferred the assets or that person's spouse receives or is entitled to receive a capital sum connected with the transfer, the income is assessible on the transferor. Any capital sum not for full consideration is covered, including a loan or loan repayment. The capital sum can be one to which a third party becomes entitled at the transferor's direction or assignment. It is not the capital sum that is taxed but the income of the overseas trust and/or company. The remarks in (a) above about the transferor's death or non-residence, apply here.

(c) Where a person not chargeable under (a) or (b) above 'receives a benefit' provided out of assets available as a result of the transfer, that person is assessible on the benefit restricted to the amount of trust income available in that year or previous years. Where the benefit exceeds the amount of income so available it is assessible in later years as income becomes available (FA 1981, s 45).

   (1) The benefit need not be received in the UK unless the beneficiary is domiciled abroad.

   (2) The benefit can be a sum to which another becomes entitled at his direction or assignment.

   (3) The same benefit cannot be assessed to both income tax and capital gains tax.

   This third provision is designed to tax the beneficiary while the first and second tax the settlor.

(d) Where an offshore income gain (FA 1984, Chap VII) accrues to an overseas trust there is no direct liability on the trust (s 96(7)) but the CGT provisions of FA 1981, s 80 are adopted to impute the gain to UK resident beneficiaries (see **6.3:2**). The result is that the resident beneficiary is assessed to income tax up to the amount of benefits received. Where both capital gains and offshore income gains could be assessed, the income tax assessment has priority.

6.3   CAPITAL GAINS TAX

Basically a non-resident trust (like a non-resident individual) is not liable to CGT (CGTA 1979, s 2(1)). The exceptions to this rule are discussed in **6.3:1** to **6.3:6**.

6.3:1   If the trust trades in the UK through a branch or agency it is liable on disposals of assets of that branch or agency – CGTA 1979, s 12.

6.3:2   If the settlor was domiciled and either resident or ordinarily resident when he made the settlement (Appendix II Note CGT 11), gains made by the trust (Appendix II Note CGT 12) can be 'imputed' to resident or ordinarily resident beneficiaries in proportion to (but not exceeding) capital payments (Appendix II Note CGT 13) received by them. The capital payments are treated as pure gain (Appendix II Note CGT 14). A non-domiciled beneficiary is excluded – FA 1981, s 80. Capital losses can be set against gains in the ordinary manner. Roll-over relief on replacement of business assets or on the transfer of a business to a company are also available. The death of a beneficiary will not affect the carry-forward of previous gains against later distributions.

But a beneficiary becoming absolutely entitled to a trust asset on a death (or otherwise) is receiving a distribution (Appendix II Note CGT 15).

6.3:3   If the settlor was domiciled and either resident or ordinarily resident at any time during the year of assessment in which the gain was made or the capital payments received the same results follow – FA 1981, s 80.

Where the settlor was non-domiciled when he made the settlement and became domiciled later, the orginal immunity will revive on his death.

6.3:4   Capital payments made before a trust became non-resident (Appendix II Note CGT 16) can be assessed under **6.3:2** or **6.3:3** above if made in anticipation of a gain to be made when non-resident (FA 1981, s 81).

6.3:5   Where a trust becomes resident after a gain is made the beneficiaries can still be assessed under **6.3:2** or **6.3:3** above if they receive capital payments.

6.3:6   Where an overseas trust holds shares in a non-resident company and gains made by the company are apportioned to its shareholders (CGTA 1979, s 15), the gains apportioned to the trust can come under **6.3:2** or **6.3:3** above (FA 1981, s 85(1)). A second charge on sale of the company's shares can be avoided if the company is liquidated within two years of the original gain (CGTA 1979, s 15(5)).

Different rules to those in **6.3:2** to **6.3:6** above apply to gains realised before 6 April 1981 and the capital payments above are those after 9 March 1981. But from 6 April 1984 discretionary capital payments can be assessed under s 80 even though the gain arose before 6 April 1981 (FA 1984, s 70).

6.3:7   Where a gain arises on a gift into an overseas trust, a 'hold-over' election can not be made (FA 1980, s 79 and FA 1982, s 82). It is possible for a trust to be UK resident for CGT but resident elsewhere under a double taxation treaty. In such circumstances a 'hold-over' election cannot be made in respect of a disposal after 17 March 1986 (FA 1986 s 58).

6.3:8   Where a 'hold-over' election has been made for a gift into a resident trust, the gain will become taxable on the trustees if the trust later becomes non-resident (FA 1981, s 79). This is an unsatisfactory state of affairs because the trust's 'cost' (reduced by the settlor's gain) is not restored to its proper value. The tax may be recovered from the settlor if the emigration occurs within six years of the year of assessment in which the disposal was made. The held-over gain becoming taxable on the trusts' emigration will be reduced by any gain realised by the trust while resident on a disposal or part disposal of the asset which was the subject of the election.

The same consequences follow if the trust becomes doubly resident after 17 March 1986.

6.3:9   The CGT exemption granted where a beneficiary disposes of his interest in a trust (CGTA 1979, s 58) does not apply after

9 March 1981 where the trust is non-resident (FA 1981, s 88).

As to whether the beneficiary's cost is nil or market value – the rule is the same as with a trust's acquisition from an excluded settlor – see Appendix II Note CGT 3.

6.3:10 The exempt gain referred to in **6.3:9** is chargeable on the trustees if the disposal is followed by the trust becoming non-resident (FA 1981, s 88(2)). The date of the taxable gain is the date of change in residence. However relief is given if the trustees sell assets while still resident.

This is another potential liability that non-resident trustees should watch out for. The Revenue can recover from the beneficiary but he in turn can recover from the trustees.

6.3:11 Where the annual exemption is being divided between trusts formed by the same settlor after 6 June 1978, a non-resident trust can be ignored.

6.4 INHERITANCE TAX

6.4:1 Basically an overseas trust is chargeable to IHT in the ordinary way. On the death of a beneficiary, for example, the value of the property in which he has an interest in possession will be chargeable irrespective of where the trust is resident. Similarly, where the settlor was UK domiciled when he made the settlement, a discretionary trust is liable to periodic charge and exit charge irrespective of where it is resident.

It is important therefore that non-resident trustees realise that their personal UK assets may be at risk.

6.4:2 However, it is not practical to apply UK tax to every asset of every trust and so exemption is granted to trust property situated outside the UK at the date of charge if the settlor was non-domiciled (Appendix III Note IHT 12) when he made the settlement. Such exempt assets are known as 'excluded property'. But here again the residence of the trust is irrelevant – even the situation of the assets is not determined by the residence of the trust.

The non-domiciled settlor is dealt with in **8.4**.

6.4:3 Exempt gilts are also excluded property if the beneficiary having an interest in possession is non-domiciled, and non-ordinarily resident. An interest in possession is not necessary if every past, present and potential beneficiary qualifies as above (Appendix III Note IHT 15).

But a discretionary trust of which all the beneficiaries qualify cannot invest in exempt gilts without an exit charge (IHTA 1984, s 65). This exit charge would only apply if the settlor were domiciled when he made the settlement.

6.4:4   A reversionary interest which was purchased can still be excluded property if the assets are situated outside the UK and the person entitled to the interest is not domiciled.

6.4:5   The specific provisions for overseas trusts are:
(a) The settlor (if alive) or any beneficiary will be liable for the trust's CTT (IHTA 1984, s 201(1)(c)).
(b) An annual charge was planned to operate on account of the periodic (ten yearly) charge, but ceased on 31 December 1981.
(c) A person concerned in making an overseas trust for a UK domiciled settlor, has a duty to disclose details to the Revenue (IHTA 1984, s 218).
(d) Foreign currency bank accounts can be exempt where there was a non-domiciled settlor – see **8.4:4**.

6.5   CONCLUSIONS

6.5:1   Introduction

At first sight an overseas trust could have many tax advantages, but a more detailed examination shows that most of the obvious advantages have been countered by legislation. However, there is still advantage to be gained from forming an overseas trust in the following circumstances.

6.5:2   Income tax

(a) Where the income of an overseas company does not arise in consequence of the transfer of assets eg the company already had the income before it was purchased by the trustees.
(b) Where the trust is to have overseas income which is to be accumulated or paid to a non-resident beneficiary.
(c) Where a resident beneficiary is not domiciled and income from overseas sources is not to be remitted to the UK.

6.5:3 Capital gains tax

(a) Where the trust is likely to realise capital gains and the beneficiaries (or some of them) are non-resident.
(b) Where the trust is likely to realise capital gains and capital payments to the beneficiaries are not contemplated eg the assets are being preserved for the next generation.
(c) Where an overseas company is likely to realise capital gains which may be apportioned to shareholders domiciled and resident in the UK. The shares in such a company should be held by an overseas trust and the gains will not be taxable unless there are actual payments to the beneficiaries (**6.3:6** and **6.3:2**).

6.5:4 Inheritance tax

Where the settlor is not domiciled when making the settlement and the beneficiary having an interest in possession is neither domiciled, resident nor ordinarily resident, and the trust assets include a foreign currency bank account (IHTA 1984, s 157).

Chapter 7 Introduction to Tax Planning

7.1   GENERAL

The use of trusts in tax planning is a vast subject, much of which is beyond the scope of this book. There are however a number of basic problems in the solution of which trusts can play a vital part – indeed there are basic problems which cannot be solved at all without using trusts.

So this chapter sets out these basic problems and suggests how the use of trusts can help to solve them. It also deals with certain pitfalls which the trustees must avoid.

7.2   INCOME TAX

7.2:1   Averaging income

A taxpayer whose income varies greatly from year to year, has a very inefficient income tax position. In one year he may pay tax at 60% and in the next he may lose his personal allowances due to an insufficiency of income.

It may be possible to overcome this problem by making him one of the beneficiaries of a discretionary trust. Income will only become his when it is paid to him and his income tax position can be greatly improved by paying or withholding trust income as his personal income rises and falls.

This result cannot be achieved if the taxpayer or his spouse is the settlor because in that case the trust income will be deemed his as it arises.

7.2:2   Using the changing incomes within a class

Within a family of children or grandchildren there are likely to be continued changes in the income tax positions of individual members. One may continue long in further education while another may commence employment as soon as possible. One may marry while another may not. One may succeed while another may become unemployed. One may give up employment to return to further education. And so on.

This is another of those circumstances in which a discretionary trust can be an ideal arrangement, enabling income to be paid to those beneficiaries who can recover all or part of the 45% tax paid by the trust.

7.2:3   Converting income to capital

Where trustees decide to accumulate income and the deed gives them power to do so, and they do not offend against the rules limiting accumulation (**1.3:2**) then the accumulated income normally becomes part of the capital for the purposes of trust law. For tax purposes, however, payments made to or for the benefit of an infant or a discretionary beneficiary are almost certainly his income even if made out of accumulated income of earlier years.

But where a beneficiary becomes absolutely entitled to capital on a contingency and in consequence he receives the accumulated income, he receives it as capital. The Revenue cannot treat it as his income in the year he becomes entitled to it nor can they go back and treat it as his income year by year as it arose.

Thus if his tax rate is higher than 45% he saves the difference on the accumulated income that he receives.

7.2:4   Getting tax relief for interest

An individual can only claim tax relief for interest paid in certain restricted circumstances. The borrowed money must have been used in his business or to buy his residence or used for a few other purposes.

If, however, the money is borrowed by a trust there will be no higher rate liability on the income used to pay the interest. In the case of a discretionary trust the interest paid will be deducted from the income before calculating the surcharge and in the case of a fixed interest trust it will be deducted before calculating the beneficiary's income for higher rate tax.

If the individual could not have obtained relief for the interest it is very unlikely that the trust will get basic rate relief – the conditions for a trust are even more restrictive than for an individual (see **2.3:2**) – thus only higher rate relief is obtained.

There is an exception where the trust income is deemed the settlor's because TA 1970, s 456 provides that the deemed income shall include any income paid out as interest (see Appendix I Note IT 16).

7.2:5   Avoiding the application of TA 1970 s 451

The best way of avoiding these provisions is to avoid any loans to or from the trust or any other capital payments to the settlor not for full consideration.

The alternative (less satisfactory) ways are:

(a) To make sure that the trust has no taxable income. This can create artificial tax liabilities if any payments are made of an income nature. It also imposes severe limits on the trustees' investment policy.

They have to invest in savings certificates, or single premium life policies, or shares that pay no dividend or other exceptional assets.

(b) To make sure that the trust has no undistributed income. This restricts the trustees' distribution policy and in particular prevents them from saving income for special needs or making use of the beneficiaries' tax positions.

(c) To give fixed interests in the trust income. This will mean a loss of flexibility and result in the assets being treated as part of the estate of each beneficiary for IHT.

7.2:6   Avoiding the application of TA 1970, s 451A

In the common case where some shares in a family company are owned by a trust it is very dangerous for the settlor or his spouse to run a current account with the company. If the company can make straightforward payments to him of the net amounts of any fees, bonuses, dividends etc to which he is entitled, many risks and difficulties can be avoided.

The alternative solutions are as set out in 7.2:5 ie

(a) Avoid capital payments from the trust to the company.

(b) The trust has no taxable income.

(c) The trust has no undistributed income.

(d) The trust has fixed interests.

7.3   CAPITAL GAINS TAX

7.3:1   Preparing for future gains

The shareholders in a family company may face the possibility of large capital gains at some future date which cannot be covered by exemptions or losses or even retirement relief. Such gains may arise on a take-over, or a disposal on the USM or The Stock Exchange.

Nor is this problem restricted to such shareholdings. A certain piece of land or some other type of property may carry a strong possibility of a large future gain.

Emigration is often the easiest solution to put forward but much harder to effect.

An overseas trust may well provide an answer so long as certain points are kept in mind:

(a) There can be no hold-over election for a gift to a non-resident and this is an argument for early action before the gain becomes too large.

(b) The arrangement may fall victim to the 'new approach' and this is another argument for early action so that the gain, when it arises, will not form part of a 'planned series of transactions'.

(c) Capital payments to beneficiaries will normally give rise to CGT (**6.3:2** and **6.3:3**) and so the arrangement is more suited to a case where the beneficiaries are non-resident or where the capital is to be preserved in the trust for the next generation.

If the gift into a discretionary trust would give rise to an unacceptable IHT liability, the CGT can still be mitigated or deferred by a fixed interest trust in which the settlor or his spouse has the interest in possession. There can however be a problem here because if CGT is paid on gains made by the non-resident trust during the settlor's interest in possession, that CGT will not be deductible in calculating the IHT on his death.

7.3:2   Avoiding CGT on resident beneficiaries

Where an overseas trust has made a capital gain, the aim should be to distribute at least the amount of the gain to non-resident beneficiaries. Distributions to resident beneficiaries should be made in the following year (or years) when there is no further gain to be apportioned to them.

7.3:3   Using the annual exempt gains

Use can be made of the fact that the settlor has an annual exemption of £6,300 and his trust (or trusts) an additional £3,150. This can be increased by having more than five trusts with £630 each. It can also be increased by husband and wife forming separate trusts.

Where investments are being gifted into trust the settlor should make sure he has used his exemption before he elects for a hold-over. For this purpose it is possible to use the exemption for certain investments and a hold-over for others.

If certain investments are likely to be sold by the trustees soon after settlement it may be possible to use the trust's exemption for these and the settlor's for the others.

Where a single asset is being settled it is possible for the settlor to put the trust in funds to give him partial consideration for the asset. This divides the gain into a part that can be held-over and a part that cannot (FA 1980, s 79(3)). The settlor's exemption can be used against the latter.

Where a beneficiary becomes absolutely entitled to investments it is again possible to use a hold-over election for some (that would produce a liability) and not for others (that would be covered by the trust's annual exemption).

7.3:4   Using the tax-free uplift on death

Death is an exempt disposal. Thus where an interest in possession ceases on a death, the assets take their market value for the purposes of a future disposal, but there is no CGT to be paid on the gain.

Where a trust asset carries a large potential gain, it may be possible to avoid the tax liability if an interest in possession can be given to an elderly person. If it is desired to give the income to a younger person it may be possible to give the interests in succession, so that the tax-free uplift arises before the younger beneficiary takes his interest.

An asset cannot be put into trust for this purpose because a gain held-over at the time of settlement will not be erased by the death of a life tenant.

Where two beneficiaries are each entitled to half the trust income for life it may be possible and sensible for the trustees to divide the assets into two separate funds with those assets showing the largest gains appropriated for the beneficiary with the shortest expectation of life.

7.3:5   Preserving capital losses

As capital gains are erased by death so are capital losses. This applies on the death of a life tenant where he was entitled to the income from the asset showing the loss.

This can be overcome by selling the asset before the death of the life tenant, and the loss will then carry forward as long as the trust lasts. Care should be taken to avoid a sale to a connected person, because in that event the loss could only be relieved against a gain on another disposal to the same person.

Losses may also be at risk when a beneficiary becomes absolutely entitled to assets on an occasion other than a death – for example an appointment or the happening of a contingency. Where the disposal of the asset (by the trustees to the beneficiary) shows a loss and the trustees can not make the use of the loss, it can be passed on to the beneficiary. What is sometimes overlooked is that an earlier loss can also be passed on if it arose in respect of property which is 'represented by the property' passing to the beneficiary (CGTA 1979, s 54 (2)). This can be the assets in which the proceeds are reinvested or even the cash itself if it has not been reinvested.

Losses should if possible be passed on to the beneficiary who can best make use of them. Thus where trustees have the power to appropriate assets to one beneficiary or another, or when they have discretion when to make appointments of assets, they should enquire into the personal CGT positions of the beneficiaries to see who can use the losses and when – a loss cannot be set against a beneficiary's gain unless he becomes entitled in the year of the gain or an earlier year. In other words the loss is deemed to have arisen at the time the asset passes to the beneficiary even if it arose to the trustees in an earlier year.

7.3:6   Secondhand hold-overs

Here we consider the position where there is a gain on a gift into trust and a beneficiary has a life interest. If on the death of the beneficiary the asset remains in trust the held-over gain becomes taxable and there is no transferee to join in an election for a second hold-over. There are two possible solutions to this problem.

(a) To so structure the trust that the asset passes to remaindermen on the death of the life tenant.

(b) If this is not possible (perhaps because the remaindermen are likely to be too young) to arrange that the asset passes to different trustees on different trusts. The second set of trustees can then join in the secondhand hold-over election.

7.4   INHERITANCE TAX

7.4:1   Equalising spouses' estates

This basic tax planning device reduces the estate of the wealthier partner, doubles the annual exemption, and doubles the zero-rate band and the lower rate bands for the purposes of trust formation. By using two donors it also increases the chances of one donor surviving for seven years. Part of this result can be achieved by the wealthier partner leaving assets to the other by will, but this depends on the partners dying in the right order and is therefore not to be recommended. However, the truth is that absolute gifts between spouses to avoid CTT were quite rare, and no doubt the same will apply to IHT. A trust can provide an effective alternative.

One spouse can gift assets free of tax into a trust in which the other has an interest in possession. In this way the settlor reduces his estate but does not use his exemptions or zero-rate band. The remaindermen would normally be the children or grandchildren.

If it is desired to use the life tenant's exemptions and zero-rate band (and its renewal after seven years) the trustees can be given power to appoint capital away from the tenant – say to the children or grandchildren. This has the same tax effect as gifts by that spouse. Some tax planners refer to her as the 'default beneficiary' because she receives the income in default of an appointment away from her.

The children (or grandchildren) should be entitled to the capital (or at least the income) on the tenant's death to avoid further tax on later appointments to them.

7.4:2   Using zero-rate band

Now that gifts to individuals are free of IHT (provided the donor survives seven years) the opportunity should be taken by those with substantial estates to make lifetime gifts before a change of government closes the door again. But here again experience teaches that absolute gifts for tax savings are not common – the prospective donor is concerned that the varying future needs of his children or grandchildren cannot be foreseen or he is just reluctant to make a firm decision as to who gets what.

Prior to 18 March 1986 discretionary trusts were used so that the settlor could be a beneficiary without the trust assets being treated as part of his estate. But extensive marketing up of 'inheritance trusts' by insurance companies has sounded the death knell of this planning tool, as it has with so many others in the past.

Thus, it is no longer possible since 18 March 1986 to remove assets from a settlor's estate while the settlor is a beneficiary of his trust. Nevertheless a discretionary trust can still be a useful device if the settlor is prepared to give up the opportunity to benefit personally. It still removes the increase in value of the assets from his estate and removes the assets entirely if he survives seven years. It allows him as a trustee to have a say in who gets what as the varying needs of his family (and their tax positions) emerge. It allows him to retain the right to appoint trust capital in his will. And there is no tax involved if he does not exceed his zero-rate band.

The settlor's home is not a suitable asset for such a trust, for it will be part of his estate as long as he resides there.

Shares in the family company are however a suitable asset, and business relief can enable larger amounts to be settled without liability. It should be remembered, however, that the trust may not be entitled to the same relief on distributions either because it does not control the company or because it has not held the shares for two years.

If no more than zero-rate band is used then any appointment by the trustees in the first ten years will probably be free of tax (But see Example **4.10:16**). On the tenth anniversary (and thereafter) any increase in the value of the assets can produce a liability but only if the increase exceeds that of the zero-rate band.

7.4:3   Using life-time rates

Having used his zero-rate band it may be sensible for the settlor to go on and use lifetime rates. If his expectation of life is in excess of seven years he can look forward to the lower rate bands renewing themselves after that period. If his expectation of life is less than seven years there may still be an advantage due to tapering relief.

Again the value of assets gifted can be increased if business or agricultural relief is available.

Different considerations apply when deciding the type of trust to be set up; because having used up his zero-rate band a discretionary trust would have liabilities on future 'transfers' even within the first ten years. And of course the settlor's taxable transfers in the seven years before the settlement will remain in the trust's 'snowball' throughout its life and not just for ten years.

There is therefore a case for a fixed interest trust if the settlor's ideas about the future have become more settled. If he still has problems then the trustees can be given overriding powers of appointment.

7.4:4   Skipping a generation

Where wealth 'skips' a generation it avoids one charge of IHT.
(a) This can be achieved by virtue of the fact that a reversionary interest is normally ignored for IHT purposes. The remainder-

man in a fixed interest trust can gift his (future) interest to his children or grandchildren without incurring any liability. The gift is also free of CGT. Once the life tenant dies this opportunity is lost.

(b) Generation skipping can of course be achieved directly by the settlor but this gives rise to problems:

    (1) grandchildren are likely to be minors;

    (2) others are likely to be born;

    (3) their future needs are unknown.

These points can be overcome by a discretionary trust but this would give rise to periodic charges and exit charges.

However, the law provides a form of trust with special privileges – an accumulation and maintenance settlement – and this avoids most of the difficulties. There is a section on such trusts (**5.1**) in the chapter on Specialised Trusts.

7.4:5   Providing cash for inheritance tax

The problem here is to provide cash which does not form part of the testators' estate and therefore does not itself become liable to tax. The simplest solution is an insurance trust – see the Chapter on Specialist Trusts (**5.5:4**).

7.4:6   Planning the life tenant's inheritance tax

A life tenant may be in the position where most of his wealth is in trust and he does not control enough capital to equalise estates or use his zero-rate band etc. If in these circumstances he wishes to do something he has two alternatives:

(a) He can persuade the trustees to distribute capital to him – this has no IHT consequence as the capital is already treated as part of his estate.

    Any capital gain can be 'held-over' by a joint election.

(b) If the terms of the trust do not permit such a distribution, or if the trustees do not see fit to make one, the life tenant can surrender his interest or part of it in favour of his children or other beneficiaries.

Note – Where the life interest was created on the death of the tenant's spouse and that death took place before 13 November 1974, the old 'surviving spouse exemption' would still operate and it would probably be disadvantageous to receive a capital distribution or surrender a life interest.

7.4:7 Preserving a high value company

Where other methods are not available or not acceptable the shares can be gifted free of IHT and CGT into an employee trust (**5.6**). The settlor and his family can retain voting control by being the trustees.

The trust can be temporary only but the shares would then be subject to a tapered IHT charge when they ceased to be held under the prescribed terms and conditions. The charge is small however starting at 1% per year of the trust's life.

At first sight this might seem a cheap method of passing shares to the next generation but some advisers believe that it is a series of transactions which could be attacked under the 'new approach'.

7.4:8 The use of separate settlements

It is a good general rule to use separate settlements wherever possible.

(a) If a discretionary trust is being set up it is well to consider whether there are different properties being settled or different classes of beneficiary being provided for. If there are, then advantage should be taken of that fact by creating separate trusts on different days. This will almost certainly reduce the future IHT burden (Example **4.10:22**).

(b) If there is to be an interest in possession in part of the trust property that part should be settled in a separate trust on a subsequent day. The separate trust will keep it out of the discretionary trust's 'transfers' and the subsequent day will keep it out of the discretionary trust's 'snowball'.

(c) If there is to be a later addition to the property of a discretionary trust this should also be the subject of a separate settlement. Added to the first trust it will suffer a periodic charge before ten years have elapsed but more seriously it can increase the trust's 'snowball' by the settlor's transfers in the seven years before the addition.

7.4:9   Simplified decision chart on type of trust

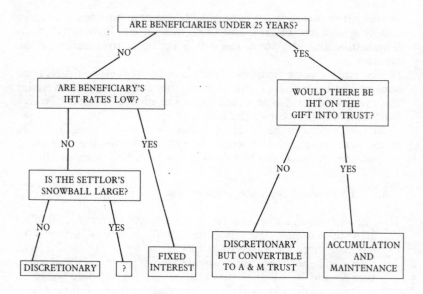

7.5   THE NEW APPROACH TO TAX AVOIDANCE

7.5:1   In view of the extent to which trusts can be used in tax planning it is appropriate to consider the 'new approach' which was adopted by the court in *W T Ramsay Ltd v IRC* [1981] STC 174, followed in *IRC v Burmah Oil Co Ltd* [1982] STC 30 and reaffirmed in *Furniss v Dawson* [1984] STC 153. It is clear that the principles involved will continue to be refined – 'the law will develop from case to case' (Lord Scarman).

7.5:2   The 'new approach' draws a distinction between a single transaction (as in *IRC v Duke of Westminster* (1935) 14 ATC 77) and a planned series of transactions (as in the *Ramsey* and *Furniss* cases) which are such as to amount to a composite transaction. Whether there is a legal obligation to carry through all the steps or whether there is just a clear intention to do so, does not appear to matter.

7.5:3   The courts then go on to make a further distinction between the form and the substance of the various steps in the plan without suggesting that any of the individual transactions are not genuine.

7.5:4 The 'new approach' can be applied when there is:

Firstly, a pre-ordained series of transactions which may or may not include the achievement of a legitimate commercial or business end.

Secondly, a step (or steps) inserted which have no commercial or business purpose apart from tax avoidance.

Where these elements are present, the courts can disregard the inserted steps when considering the application of the Taxes Acts.

7.5:5 Examples of the schemes which have fallen victim to the 'new approach' are:

(a) A scheme to get CGT relief for a loss on a loan to a subsidiary company by subscribing for shares in the subsidiary and attaching the loss to those shares (Burmah).

(b) A scheme to defer CGT on the sale of shares in a private company by forming a holding company to take the shares in exchange for its own. The new company then sold to the outside buyer. (*Furniss v Dawson* [1984] STC 153).

(c) A scheme to avoid income tax on an employee's bonus by arranging a loan to him with interest paid in advance which could be relieved against the bonus. Another company immediately took over the loan and responsibility for the interest (*Cairns v MacDiarmid* [1983] STC 178).

7.5:6 At the time of writing there have been three cases before the High Court where the judge has refused to follow *Furniss v Dawson* because the final purchaser was not in contemplation at the time of the preliminary 'inside' transaction. These cases are *Craven v White* (1985) Times, 6 June, *IRC v Bowater Property Developments Ltd* (1985) Times, 23 October and *Bayliss v Gregory* (1985) Times, 2 December. Revenue appeals in all these cases are expected to be heard early in 1987.

7.5:7 It will be appreciated that none of the above schemes involved a trust, but there is no doubt that schemes involving trusts will be subject to the same new approach. It will also be appreciated that the tax legislation has been altered since the above schemes were devised.

7.5:8 Conclusions

(a) One should approach artificial tax avoidance schemes with caution and particularly any steps in a scheme which have no other purpose.

(b) One should make sure that each transaction in a series has a genuine business purpose even though there is also a tax saving purpose.
(c) One should do one's tax planning well in advance so that the final disposal/capital transfer cannot be treated as part of a composite transaction.

Chapter 8   The Non-Domiciled Settlor

8.1   General

8.2   Income tax

8.3   Capital gains tax

8.4   Inheritance tax

8.5   Planning

8.1   GENERAL

A trust is not an individual and does not therefore have a domicile. However, the individual settlor has a domicile and this has considerable importance in all three taxes.

As non-domiciled clients are rare in the average accountant's practice, the provisions which depend on the settlor being such a person have been omitted from the main text and are here gathered into one chapter.

8.2   INCOME TAX

8.2:1   Where the settlor is non-domiciled in the year in which overseas trust income is deemed to be his under TA 1970, Pt XVI, Chaps III or IV, it can only be assessed on him on a remittances basis. This exemption does not apply to Chap II (settlements on children).

8.2:2   Where an overseas trust owns shares in a non-resident 'close' company, and undistributed income of that company is deemed income of the trust, it cannot be deemed the income of a non-domiciled settlor.

8.2:3   Where the settlor was non-domiciled and non-resident when he made the settlement the Revenue will not seek to assess the overseas income of an overseas trust on a single UK resident trustee.

8.3   CAPITAL GAINS TAX

8.3:1   Where a non-domiciled settlor gifts into trust an asset situated outside the UK he is not receiving anything in the nature of a remittance and so there is no CGT liability. This is important where the settlor is resident or ordinarily resident.

8.3:2   Where the settlor was non-domiciled when he made his gift into a non-resident trust, gains made by the trustees cannot be apportioned to the beneficiaries as long as the settlor remains non-domiciled.

8.3:3   Where the settlor becomes domiciled and the trust loses its exempt status, it will again become exempt on the settlor's death.

8.3:4 Where a settlor was not domiciled, not resident and not ordinarily resident when he made the gift into trust, the fact that the trust has a professional trustee resident in the UK and that the trust is administered in the UK will not make the trust resident for CGT purposes.

8.4 INHERITANCE TAX

8.4:1 Where the settlor was non-domiciled when he made his gift into trust, property situated outside the UK will be exempt from tax for as long as the trust lasts. This refers of course to property outside the UK at the date of charge.

8.4:2 There is an exception to this rule if the settlor or his spouse has an interest in possession from the settlement date. In that case the tenant must be non-domiciled when the interest in possession (or the second of the two) ceases – IHTA 1984, ss 80 and 82.

8.4:3 Where a discretionary trust of which all the beneficiaries are non-domiciled and non-ordinarily resident invests in exempt gilts there is an exit charge. This exit charge does not apply if the settlor was not domiciled when he made the settlement.

8.4:4 Foreign currency bank accounts are exempt on a death if, in addition to the settlor being not domiciled when he made the settlement, the beneficiary having an interest in possession is also not domiciled, not resident and not ordinarily resident.

8.5 PLANNING

8.5:1 Avoiding CGT on overseas gains

The non-domiciled but resident taxpayer who is likely to realise a gain on the disposal of an overseas asset should consider gifting the asset into trust. As the settlor's CGT liability is on a remittances basis there will be no tax. The trust acquires the asset at market value so that on a sale by the trustees the liability should be small.

8.5:2 Creating excluded property

Where the settlor is non-domiciled, UK property can become excluded if it is transferred to an overseas company, but a tax liability on the transfer has to be considered. This liability would not apply if the transfer were made by a discretionary trust (IHTA 1984, s 65(7)).

8.5:3 Preserving excluded property

A non-domiciled person who owns UK property through an overseas company may be approaching the time when he will have been UK resident for 17 years and therefore treated as domiciled. Such a person should settle the shares in the overseas company before he is deemed UK domiciled so that the shares will remain excluded property. Whether he can reserve any benefit is not yet clear.

Like all tax planning, such action should be taken early, because if the settlor were held to be domiciled when he made his gift into trust there could be a large tax liability.

8.5:4 Defence in case of doubtful domicile

Where an attempt is being made to preserve excluded property by settling it but the prospective settlor's domicile is in doubt, a liability to IHT will not arise if the settlor or his spouse has an immediate interest in possession. This however defers the date at which domicile is relevant to the end of the interest in possession and it is the domicile of the tenant that is then considered. Where husband and wife have successive interests in possession it is the end of the second interest and the domicile of the second tenant at that date that is relevant.

Where the settlor's spouse is definitely non-domiciled, that spouse should therefore have an interest in possession at the end of which the trust should become discretionary. The excluded property will then remain so for as long as the trust lasts.

Appendix I Income Tax Notes

NOTE IT 1 (See 2.1)

The reliefs due to individuals to which trusts are not entitled include:
(a) Relief for losses on unquoted shares in trading companies (FA 1980, s 37).
(b) Relief for investment in corporate trades (FA 1981, s 52).

NOTE IT 2 (See 2.2:8)

FA 1985, Sch 23, paras 6-9 apply the 'accrued income scheme' to trusts. This is the legislation directed against bondwashing.

Where there is a deemed addition to the trust's income as a result of a sale and the application of the 'accrual' principle there is a tax liability at basic rate plus investment income surcharge (a total of 45% at present rates).

In the case of a discretionary trust this tax can be brought into credit for the purposes of FA 1973, s 17.

In the case of a fixed interest trust the deemed addition will not form part of the beneficiary's income and so will not suffer higher rates. Presumably that is why the surcharge is applied to all trusts and not just discretionary trusts.

NOTE IT 3 (See 2.2:9)

FA 1984, s 100 applies the provisions of Chap VII (Offshore income gains) to trusts. Where such a gain accrues to a trust there is a liability under Schedule D Case VI at basic rate plus investment income surcharge (a total of 45% at present rates).

In the case of a discretionary trust, this tax can be brought into credit for the purposes of FA 1973, s 17.

In the case of a fixed interest trust, as the gain is income 'for all the purposes of the Tax Acts' (FA 1984, s 96 (1)) the beneficiary can presumably get credit for the tax paid.

NOTE IT 4 (See 2.3:4)

Deductible expenses are those properly chargeable to income under trust law. Broadly speaking, expenditure for the benefit of the whole estate is capital. In the cases of *Carver v Duncan* [1984] STC 556 and *Bosanquet v Allen* (1984) Times, 24 July the following were held not deductible:
(a) Premiums on the settlor's life (a gift protection policy).
(b) Fees to investment advisors.
(c) Premiums under a comprehensive insurance policy.
Provisions in the trust deed and the treatment of payments in the trust accounts are both ignored.

NOTE IT 5 (See 2.7)

The income to be treated as the settlors is extended by TA 1970, s 454 (1) to include:
(a) Income which would have been chargeable if it had been received in the UK by a person domiciled, resident and ordinarily resident there. But if the settlor himself is not domiciled or not resident or not ordinarily resident the normal exceptions will apply.
(b) Income apportioned to the trust from a close company.

NOTE IT 6 (See 2.7:1)

Where income is paid for the benefit of an unmarried infant child of the settlor the 'deeming' provision does not apply if the settlor is dead. The provisions can apply where an interest in possession is released to an unmarried infant. (*D'Abreu v IRC* [1978] STC 538).

Because of the 'deeming' provision it is normal for trusts in favour of infants to be settled by other relations – eg grandparents. If a parent has to be the settlor the settlement should be irrevocable and the deed should provide for accumulation of income so that the 'deeming' does not apply unless there are actual payments.

NOTE IT 7 (See 2.7:2)

If a power of revocation or a discretionary power which could result in capital or income reverting to the settlor (or his spouse) cannot be exercised for six years from the date property was first put into the trust, then the 'deeming' provisions do not apply until that power of revocation or discretion can be exercised – TA 1970, s 446 (1) proviso.

NOTE IT 8 (See 2.7:3)

Where IHT on the gift into trust is to be paid by the trustees this is not treated as an interest retained by the settlor (SP 1/82). It may be desirable to have such a provision in the trust to allow IHT to be payable by instalments or to avoid 'grossing up'. Note however that payment of IHT could be a capital sum applied for the settlor's benefit (TA 1970, s 451).

SP 1/82 does not appear to cover payment of CGT on the gift into trust and this is another argument in favour of claiming 'hold-over'.

NOTE IT 9 (See 2.7:3 and 2.7:4)

The 'deeming' provisions will not operate if the settlor can only benefit in any of the following circumstances:
(a) The bankruptcy of a beneficiary.
(b) A charge or assignment of his interest by a beneficiary.
(c) The death of both parties to a marriage and any children of the marriage.
(d) The death of a beneficiary of a super trust before attaining the specified age.

In addition to the above the 'deeming' provisions cannot operate while some person is alive and under 25 during whose lifetime the settlor cannot benefit TA 1970, s 447 (2) proviso.

NOTE IT 10 (See 2.7:4)

The settlor's spouse does not include his widow(er) but does include a spouse he may marry.

NOTE IT 11 (See 2.7:5)

The capital sum paid to the settlor (or his spouse) can be a loan, a loan repayment or any other capital payment not for full consideration.

The exclusion of capital payments made for full consideration does not apply to the loan or the loan repayment. Thus it does not matter that the loan is on a commercial basis as regards interest and other terms.

If the capital sum exceeds the undistributed income of the year of payment plus that of previous years it can be 'matched' with undistributed income of following years but not after the earliest of:

(a) The tenth year after the year of payment.
(b) The year the loan is fully repaid (where the capital sum is a loan to the settlor).
(c) The year the settlor dies.

Where the balance of a capital payment has been carried forward any further assessments on the settlor are in the years in which the future 'matched' income arises and not in the years of the original payment.

Where the capital sum is a loan to the settlor, the repayment of the loan does not entitle the settlor to recover any of the tax paid.

There will however be credit for the amount treated as the settlor's income against a later loan. Thus a later loan will only give rise to 'matched' income to the extent that it exceeds the income 'matched' in respect of the earlier loan.

In the reverse circumstances – where the capital sum is the repayment to the settlor of a loan by him – the same rules apply suitably adapted. No assessments can be made on the settlor for a year after he has made a later loan to the trust of at least the amount repaid.

The expression 'matched' is used instead of 'deemed' because the trust will still be liable to investment income surcharge on such income.

The calculation of 'available' income which may be 'matched' is shown in Example **2.8:14**.

NOTE IT 12 (See 2.7:5)

Where a capital sum is paid by the trust to a close company in which the trust is a participator, the anti-avoidance provision is extended to cover capital sums paid by the company to the settlor or his spouse.

This involves a double 'matching'. The first stage is to 'match' the payments by the company to the settlor with the payments from the trust to the company. If the former exceeds the latter the excess is carried forward and matched with later payments from the trust. The second stage is to 'match' the result with the available trust income as in Note IT 11 above. Payments from the trust to the company are extended to cover payments to:

(a) A non-resident 'close' company in which the trust is a participator.
(b) A company controlled by the close company or the non-resident 'close' company.
(c) A company associated with the company making the payment to the settlor.

A payment from the trust to the company is excluded if:

(a) It is not a loan or a loan repayment and is made for full value (eg a subscription for shares).
(b) It is not made within five years before or after the payment from the company to the settlor.

A payment from the company to the settlor is excluded if:

(a) It is a loan which is wholly repaid within 12 months and such loans have not been outstanding for more than 12 months in any period of 5 years.
(b) It is a loan repayment which is relent within 12 months.
(c) It is not a loan or a loan repayment and is made for full value.
(d) It has been treated as the settlor's income under the corporation tax legislation (TA 1970, s 287).

NOTE IT 13 (See 6.2:1(c))

Where a non-qualifying life policy is issued after 13 November 1983 by a non-resident company the gain is liable to basic rate as well as higher rate tax. FA 1984, Sch 15, para 8 gives relief for a period when the policyholder was non-resident. This relief is not available where the policyholder is an overseas trust.

However, if the policy was issued before 19 March 1985 and was at that date held by an overseas trust, relief is still given.

NOTE IT 14 (See 6.2:4)

Overseas income is assessed on a remittance basis where the taxpayer is:

(a) Not domiciled in the UK.
(b) A British subject or a citizen of the Republic of Ireland who is not ordinarily resident in the UK (TA 1970, s 122 (2)).

But income arising in the Republic of Ireland is exceptional in that it is always assessed on the amount arising whether remitted or not.

NOTE IT 15 (See 6.2:11)

'Power to enjoy' income may be by the successive exercise by whomsoever of a series of powers. Thus it is defined in the widest possible terms and does not merely apply where the transferor can control the application of the income. It will apply where income increases the value of the transferor's assets or might provide any other benefit to him.

NOTE IT 16 (See 7.2:4)

For the purposes of TA 1970 Pt XVI, Chap III interest paid cannot be deducted in arriving at the undistributed income of the trust in a year when no income payments were made other than to the settlor or his spouse.

Where income has been paid to another beneficiary or beneficiaries, such a proportion of the interest paid can be deducted as those income payments bear to the whole of the trust income. The whole of the trust income is after deduction of expenses but not interest.

NOTE IT 17 (See 2.6:7)

Where a beneficiary of a discretionary trust is resident in a country which has a double taxation agreement with the UK, the terms of the agreement can affect UK tax relief as follows:
(a) Where the agreement provides for a withholding tax in respect of a certain class of income (eg 15% of interest payments) the Revenue will repay to the beneficiary the excess tax on the interest content of the discretionary payment (normally the difference between 15% and 45%).
(b) Where the agreement provides that 'other income' shall be taxable only in the country of residence there will be no need to operate the 'look-through' principle and the Revenue will repay all the tax suffered (SP3/86).
(c) Where the agreement does not give sole taxing rights in respect of 'other income' to the country of residence the Revenue will operate the 'look-through' principle.
(d) The 'look-through' principle will similarly apply where the 'other income' article specifically excludes income from trusts.

Appendix II Capital Gains Tax Notes

NOTE CGT 1 (See **3.1**)

A 'chargeable asset' is any asset not specifically exempted. The asset does not have to be in the UK. The principal exemptions affecting trusts are:
(a) Certain dwelling houses (see **3.9**).
(b) Government stocks and company bonds in certain circumstances.
(c) A chattel not exceeding £3,000 at acquisition and disposal.
(d) A chattel which is a wasting asset and not used in a trade.
(e) A life policy (unless bought by the trust).

NOTE CGT 2 (See **3.1**)

A 'chargeable disposal' is a sale, a vesting, a gift or the receipt of compensation and includes a partial disposal.

A disposal on death is exempt as is one between spouses and one to charity. So is compensation spent on restoration or (if elected) on replacement.

NOTE CGT 3 (See **3.2:3** and **6.3:9**)

Between 10 March 1981 and 5 April 1983 the trust's acquisition value was nil if the settlor was an excluded person – ie he was not resident and not ordinarily resident (FA 1981, s 90 (1)). For transactions after 5 April 1983 the normal market value rule is brought in by FA 1984, s 66. Between 6 April 1983 and 5 April 1985 there could be a joint election to retain the 1981 rule in cases where the excluded person was (exceptionally) liable on his disposal.

NOTE CGT 4 (See **3.3:2**)

Annual exemptions have been increased as follows:

	Individuals	Trusts	Minimum
1980/81	3,000	1,500	300
1981/82	3,000	1,500	300
1982/83	5,000	2,500	500
1983/84	5,300	2,650	530
1984/85	5,600	2,800	560
1985/86	5,900	2,950	590

NOTE CGT 5 (See **3.3:4**)

The persons connected with the settlor and therefore to the trust are:
(a) The settlor's spouse.
(b) Any brother, sister, ancestor or lineal descendent of settlor or spouse.
(c) Any spouse of any of the above.
(d) Any partner of the settlor.
(e) Any associate as above of any such partner.
(f) Any company controlled by the settlor with his connected persons.

NOTE CGT 6 (See **3.4:4**)

The consequences of the exercise by trustees of a power of appointment are dealt with in a Revenue statement of practice (SP 7/84). Broadly this confirms that if the assets over which the power is exercised remain in the trust there is no deemed disposal. Even if fresh trusts are created by the appointment there will be no deemed disposal provided the appointment is revocable or that the assets may in some other way come to be held in the future under the original terms of the trust.

NOTE CGT 7 (See **3.5:1 and 3.5:3**)

Where the beneficiary who takes the asset is resident in the UK and a 'hold-over' election is made, the gain becomes taxable if the beneficiary becomes non-resident within six years of assessment after the year of the disposal to him. If the beneficiary does not pay this

CGT within 12 months the trustees are liable for it and they should therefore look for some form of security before signing the hold-over election.

NOTE CGT 8 (See 3.8:2)

The fact that the trustees are liable to CGT on the increase in the value of the trust assets is the reason why the beneficiary is not liable to CGT on the increase in the value of his interest. The two increases may in reality be one.

Thus where a beneficiary is liable because he had purchased his interest there is a form of double taxation not unlike that which applies to a company shareholder whose gains are derived from his company's gains. This position may make the purchase of a beneficial interest a relatively poor bargain.

NOTE CGT 9 (See 3.8:2)

The rule that a disposal of a beneficiary's interest is chargeable if it was acquired for valuable consideration is itself subject to an exception. This is where it was acquired for consideration consisting of another interest under the settlement (CGTA 1979, s 58 (1)). This exception allows the terms of the trust to be varied without the beneficiary's interest becoming a chargeable asset.

NOTE CGT 10 (See 6.1)

The status of a non-resident trust is extended to one with a UK resident professional trustee where all the trust property was provided by a person who, when he settled the property was neither domiciled, resident nor ordinarily resident in the UK (CGTA 1979, s 52 (2)). In these circumstances the administration of the trust is deemed to be carried on abroad. This is to encourage foreigners to use UK professional skills.

NOTE CGT 11 (See 6.3:2)

The income tax definition of settlement to include any 'agreement or arrangement' as set out in TA 1970, s 454 (3) is adopted by FA 1981, s 83 (7).

NOTE CGT 12 (See **6.3:2**)

Gains made by the trust can include gains apportioned from a non-resident 'close' company in which the trust holds shares.

NOTE CGT 13 (See 6.3:2)

Capital payments which can be assessed to CGT in the hands of beneficiaries of overseas trusts are payments not chargeable to income tax or, if the beneficiary is a non-resident, payments received otherwise than as income (CGTA 1979, s 83(1)). They include assets transferred and other benefits but it would seem that a loan on a commercial basis is excluded (CGTA 1979, s 83(4)). An interest-free loan repayable on demand may well have a very low value. They also include payments applied for his benefit or at his direction (CGTA 1979, s 83(5)).

NOTE CGT 14 (See **6.3:2**)

The apportionment of gains is on a strictly arithmetical basis without regard to the status of the beneficiary. Both gains and capital payments can be carried forward for 'matching' in later years.

	Trust Gains	Beneficiaries		
		A	B	C
1984/85 Trust's gains	50,000			
1985/86 Capital payments		15,000	15,000	—
Gains apportioned	(30,000)	(15,000)	(15,000)	—
Gains forward	20,000	—	—	—
1986/87 Capital payments		10,000	10,000	20,000
Gains apportioned	(20,000)	(5,000)	(5,000)	(10,000)
Payments forward		5,000	5,000	10,000

If A is resident, B is not resident and C resident but not domiciled this will not affect the apportionment of the gains but will mean that only A is assessible.

NOTE CGT 15 (See **6.3:2**)

Where a beneficiary becomes absolutely entitled to trust assets this is treated as a distribution for the purpose of FA 1981, s 80. This has the unfortunate effect of rendering him liable to CGT on unattributed gains up to the value of the assets he becomes entitled to. Where he is sole remainderman he may be liable on all the gains realised while the trust has been non-resident.

If the occasion is the death of the life tenant, unrealised gains will be erased.

NOTE CGT 16 (See **6.3:4**)

Extra-statutory concession A 11 which allows an individual to be treated as non-resident from the date of departure, does not apply to trusts. A trust is resident or not resident for the full tax year.

Appendix III Inheritance Tax Notes

NOTE IHT 1 (See **4.1:9** (b))

'Excluded property' is property excluded from the scope of IHT, that is to say there is no charge when an interest in possession in such property ceases. Also it cannot be relevant property for the purposes of a periodic charge or an exit charge. The property concerned is:

(a) Assets situated outside the UK where the settlor was domiciled (Note IHT 12 below) outside the UK when he made the settlement.

(b) A 'reversionary interest' – see Note IHT 3 below.

(c) Exempt gilts where the person having an interest in possession is neither domiciled nor ordinarily resident in the UK. An interest in possession is not required if every past, present and potential beneficiary qualifies as above.

NOTE IHT 2 (See **4.3:2**)

A beneficiary of a trust has an 'interest in possession' in a trust asset if he is absolutely and currently entitled to the income. Or looked at from the other side, the trustees have no right to withhold the income or to accumulate it. The right of rent-free occupation of a house is normally an interest in possession (see SP 10/79). It is 'a present right to present enjoyment of the property' – *Pearson v IRC* [1980] STC 318.

There is a rare exception to this rule when trustees are required to accumulate income which must in the end go to the beneficiary or to his estate if he is dead. Thus there must be no contingency such as reaching a certain age or surviving a certain person, but a certainty that the beneficiary will eventually be entitled to the accumulations. Beyond establishing the existence of this exceptional case we need not spend more time on it. It follows the rules for 'interest in possession'.

In view of the repeated references to 'the person having an interest in possession' the shortened description of 'tenant' has been adopted.

NOTE IHT 3 (See **4.3:9** and **4.7:1**)

A 'reversionary interest' (or an interest in expectancy) is a future interest in a trust – the most common being the interest which will arise on the death of a life tenant.

Such an interest is excluded property (not liable to IHT) unless:
(a) It was purchased. But if the property is situated outside the UK and the person entitled to the reversionary interest is not domiciled in the UK it does not matter that it was purchased.
(b) It will arise on the determination of a lease for life not granted for full consideration. This is because the full value of the property is not treated as part of the lessee's estate.
(c) The reversioner is the settlor or his spouse and the settlement was made after 15 April 1976. This is because the value of the settlor's gift into trust took account of the reversion.

NOTE IHT 4 (See **4.3:10**)

Where a settlement has no trustees IHTA 1984, s 45 provides that any person in whom the trust property or its management is vested shall be a trustee.

NOTE IHT 5 (See 4.4:1)

'Relevant property' is trust assets in which there is no 'interest in possession' (Note IHT 2 above). It does not however include assets held for charitable purposes, for maintaining historic buildings, for a superannuation fund, for an employees' trust, for a disabled persons' trust, for a trade compensation fund, for an accumulation and maintenance trust (a super trust **5.1:1**) or assets which are 'excluded property' (Note IHT 1 above).

NOTE IHT 6 (see **4.4:1** and **4.5:2**)

The 'transfers' out of relevant property (Note IHT 5 above) are as follows:

(a) Where relevant property leaves the trust. Note that there is no exemption when relevant property reverts to the settlor – this exemption only applies to property in which there was a fixed interest.

(b) Where any person takes an interest in possession (Note IHT 2 above) in what was relevant property.

(c) Where the terms of the trust are altered with the result that what was relevant property becomes subject to the terms of an accumulation and maintenance settlement (a super trust **5.1:1**).

NOTE IHT 7 (See **4.5:7**)

A settlor is defined in IHTA 1984, s 44 to include any person by whom the settlement was made directly or indirectly and includes any person who has provided funds directly or indirectly in connection with the settlement. Where a settlement has more than one settlor it may be treated as more than one settlement.

NOTE IHT 8 (See **4.6:4**)

A 'related trust' is one which was formed on the same day by the same settlor. Such a trust is however ignored if it is an unlimited charitable trust.

NOTE IHT 9 (See **4.7:2 (a)**)

The first periodic charge is on the first ten-year anniversary falling after 31 March 1983, but there is an exception if a payment was made out of the trust during the year ending 31 March 1984 which could not have been made without an application to court. Where that applies the payment out is not charged by the device of postponing the first charge to 1 April 1984 if it would otherwise have fallen before that date. The dates of later charges are not affected.

NOTE IHT 10 (See **4.8:1**)

A disposal of an interest in possession is not treated as a transfer if it is made:

(a) By one spouse for the maintenance of the other.

(b) For the maintenance or training of a child of either party (or an illegitimate child of the disposer or another child not in the care of his parent) who is a minor or undergoing full-time training.
(c) As a reasonable provision for the care or maintenance of a dependant relative of the disposer.

NOTE IHT 11 (See **4.8:8**)

Qualifying property for the purposes of payment by instalments is:
(a) Land.
(b) Shares giving control to the trustees and the person having an interest in possession, together. Where there is no interest in possession, to the trustees alone.
(c) Unquoted shares not giving control. This item is the subject of complicated rules.
(d) A business or an interest in a business.

NOTE IHT 12 (See **6.4:2**)

Where a settlement was made after 9 December 1974 a settlor shall be treated as UK domiciled when he made a settlement if:
(a) he was UK domiciled within three years before that date but not if he was not UK domiciled at any time after 9 December 1974, or
(b) he was UK resident for 17 of the 20 years of assessment ending with the year of settlement but not if he was not UK resident at any time after 9 December 1974. A dwelling house available for use shall be ignored in determining residence (IHTA 1984, s 267).

NOTE IHT 13 (See **5.7:1**)

Property in a newspaper trust other than shares in a newspaper publishing company must be reasonably required to secure the operation of the newspaper publishing company (IHTA 1984, s 87 (3)).

NOTE IHT 14 (See 4.1:11)

Whether the amount charged has to be grossed up or not depends on whether the tax is paid out of the amount charged or out of other trust property. The amount charged does not fall to be grossed up where:

(a) An interest in possession in the whole trust property ceases.
(b) An interest in possession in part of the trust property ceases and the tax is repayable out of that part.
(c) A periodic charge is made on a discretionary trust.
(d) An exit charge is made on a discretionary trust and the tax is payable out of the property ceasing to be relevant.

There is a grossing up of the amount charged where:

(a) An interest in possession in part of the trust property ceases and the tax is payable out of other trust property.
(b) An exit charge is made on a discretionary trust and the tax is payable out of other trust property.

NOTE IHT 15 (See 6.4:3)

It was held in *Minden Trust (Cayman) Ltd v IRC* [1984] STC 434 that in a discretionary trust it is not sufficient to look at the beneficiaries potentially interested in the exempt gilts. One must look at all the beneficiaries potentially interested in any property of the trust.

NOTE IHT 16 (See 4.8:4 and 4.8:5)

Where the estate of a deceased or a transfer attracts business relief or agricultural relief and is also partly exempt (because, for example, part goes to the spouse) there is a particular problem regarding the incidence of the relief.

Until 17 March 1986 the relief is given first and then the exempt part of the estate or the transfer is ascertained.

For transfers after 17 March 1986 where there is a specific gift of property qualifying for relief then the relief will attach to that property. In other cases the relief will be allocated pro rata between the chargeable and exempt parts of the estate or the transfer (FA 1986, s 105).

Index

155